The New Masters of REAL ESTATE

Published by CelebrityPress™, Orlando, FL
A division of The Celebrity Branding Agency®

Celebrity Branding® is a registered trademark
Printed in the United States of America.

ISBN: 9780982908303
LCCN: 2010933437

This publication is designed to provide accurate and authoritative information with regard to the subject matter covered. It is sold with the understanding that the publisher is not engaged in rendering legal, accounting, or other professional advice. If legal advice or other expert assistance is required, the services of a competent professional should be sought. The opinions expressed by the authors in this book are not endorsed by CelebrityPress™ and are the sole responsibility of the author rendering the opinion.

Most CelebrityPress™ titles are available at special quantity discounts for bulk purchases for sales promotions, premiums, fundraising, and educational use. Special versions or book excerpts can also be created to fit specific needs.

For more information, please write:

CelebrityPress™,
520 N. Orlando Ave, #44,
Winter Park, FL 32789

or call 1.877.261.4930

Visit us online at www.**CelebrityPressPublishing**.com

The New Masters of REAL ESTATE

Getting Deals DONE in the New Economy

TABLE OF CONTENTS:

FOREWORD

In my 30 years of buying and selling houses and 25 years teaching others how to do it correctly, I've seen a lot of folks enter our world of low risk real estate investing. Among them, a certain percentage quickly rise to the top and excel. They 'stand out from the herd' because they make more money than most, in less time and with less work.

There are very good reasons for this, the most important being a dogged determination to succeed no matter what. However, there's another trait they all have in common…the willingness to follow instructions and hitch their wagon to qualified advice from those who've 'been there and done that', not just give it 'lip service.'

Everyone in this book is in this group. They are all leaders who proved their worth, got good at what they do and most importantly, are willing to share it with you. All of them came from ordinary jobs and professions, discovered real estate, got the proper training and then 'put the pedal to the metal.'

This book is full of leaders who've been there, done that and come out on top - despite all the 'dream stealers' trying to pull them down.

They are survivors, many overcoming large obstacles, both physical and financial, and a few mental roadblocks as well.

You've never seen a book like this. It's not fiction or entertainment. For many it will be the beginning of a new lifestyle.

The lessons in this book would take years to learn, possibly a lifetime or maybe never. Reading it is like sitting in the middle of a table in a brainstorming meeting – attended by some of the best minds in real estate.

I'd consider you lucky to have discovered this book. Sit down in a quiet place and get to know your authors, and when you see them in 'live trainings' let them know how much you appreciate their contribution.

To your Quantum Leap,

Ron Holland

PREFACE

WHO IS RON LEGRAND AND HOW CAN HE CHANGE YOUR LIFE
By Ron LeGrand

When I first got involved with Real Estate, I was a dead broke auto mechanic trying to make enough money to make ends meet. There was no such thing as a disposable income around my house. It was all disposed of before I got it. Thirty-five-years-old and bankrupt, I didn't have a clue what I wanted to be when I grew up; but I knew it wasn't fixing cars in the hot Florida sun.

The year was 1982. I saw an ad that said something like "Come learn how to buy real estate with no money or credit and get rich by next Thursday." That appealed to me because I had no money or credit and I kinda liked the rich idea. So I attended the seminar.

The instructor got us all excited about real estate and showed us how people were buying real estate with no money down. Then he said that if you paid $450 and attend our two-day training this weekend, we'll show you the secrets. I wanted in but I had a big problem-actually 450 big problems.

But something compelled me to find a way to get the money, and that's what I did. I borrowed it from two friends and showed up for the seminar. That decision changed my life forever, my family's life, and their family's lives for generations to come, not to mention hundreds of thousands of my students and their descendants into the millions. That one small split-second decision that could have gone either way made me millions of dollars and spawned countless numbers of millionaires all over North America, Canada and in many countries I can't even pronounce.

In fact, most of the stuff taught in that seminar was over my head. I was clueless and could barely spell real estate. But I picked up the idea I felt I could use, and within three weeks I made my first $3,000 from real estate using no money or credit, as I had none of either. I immediately called my boss and said "I'm upping my income....see you around!"

The biggest thing that seminar did was get me involved in real estate and, committed to changing my lifestyle. For years I'd been looking for something but didn't know what it was. When I got my hands on that three grand, it became crystal clear that real estate was my future.

Fast-forward two years: I had amassed 276 units-some single family, some apartments-not including some I sold along the way to live. I was a millionaire...on paper. I had over $1 million in equity two years after I started with no money or credit.

REALITY ARRIVES!

I sat down one Friday evening to pay my bills and realized my outgo was bigger than my income and my upkeep was becoming my downfall. All I had accomplished was creating a big ugly mess. I'd spent two years buying the wrong properties the wrong ways in the wrong areas for the wrong reasons. I built my empire on a house of cards not a solid foundation.

You see, I really didn't understand the real estate business. I just bought properties because I could without money or credit. I bought all the crap savvy investors wouldn't touch. They'd already been to the school I was about to graduate from- "The School of Hard Knocks." All my low-income properties in war zone areas with brainless tenants were sucking me dry, financially and mentally. My days were spent solving these tenants' petty problems and listening to all the worthless reasons why they couldn't pay rent.

I spent the next five years selling all my junk for dimes on the dollar. It took me seven years in the business to really understand it and get my life back. Oh, I made a good living during that time several times my previous income-but I sure wish I'd have known myself back then and had the system my students have now. On second thought, it wouldn't have mattered anyway. I wouldn't have listened. I'm a man and men don't follow instructions. It's the way we're wired.

After about seven years in the business and over 400 houses later, I built an easy system to turn real estate in to cash immediately, cash monthly, and cash later. I made it a real business anyone could operate from home to make obscene amounts of money. That's about the time I started teaching what I had learned. Somewhere along the line someone called me "The World's Leading Expert at Quick Turning Houses" and the name stuck.

In the 1990's the information company I built went public with revenues exceeding $20 million annually from my books, tapes, and seminars.

Now fast-forward a few more years of teaching what I know while simultaneously doing what I teach, and I will admit I'm a weird dude. I have bought and sold over 2,000 houses and still do 2 or 3 a month with an average profit of $40,000 with the help of my Executive Assistant, who spends 10 to 15 hours a week at real estate.

Over the years I've created a mountain of home study products; written millions of words in print; and shared the platform with past presidents, movie stars, actors, politicians, sports heroes, business leaders, super wealthy individuals from all professions, and some of the best speakers in the world. I've spoken to audiences as small as 20 and as large as 20,000 in hotel meeting rooms and coliseums all across North America. I've gazed in amazement and sheer joy as so many thousands of my clients and new friends have pulled themselves out of mediocrity, or downright poverty, and made themselves financially independent millionaires and some even multi-millionaires from the words that left my lips and the time spent together.

So many of these new millionaires have now become leaders reaching out to hand to those in need, to help them climb the ladder to success like the ones in this book. My legacy has spread like a swarm of locusts, and millions will be affected or already have been by the positive impact I made with a few carefully chosen words that left my lips or published in print at a time when students were ready to receive them and convert them to action. New generations will profit directly or indirectly from the words in this book because they attended one of my seminars, then used the information and passed it on. *When the student is ready, the teacher will appear.*

Much of my time now is spent in front of good people who are serious about getting rich and will do what it takes to become one of the three percent who can not only say but prove they have achieved true wealth. People constantly ask me why I continue to teach. It's hard for them to understand why a multimillionaire would take time to work with those who aren't.

My answer is simple, really. First, make no mistake about it; I get paid well for teaching. It's not a mercy mission, and we're not a non-profit organization. Second, I have to do something with my time; golf, fishing, and diving get old quickly. Making millionaires never gets old, and I can't think of anything I would rather do with my life. It's fun to be me and I love doing it.

Besides, I've been married over 45 years to one woman. Her name is Beverly and between the Honey Do's (her request) and the nine grandchildren (three live on our estate), it's nice to get away once in a while. Beverly says that even though we have been married over 45 years, it's closer to 3 if you take out the travel time.

Truthfully, I'm just a simple auto mechanic with a redneck background who barely got out of high school. I'd rather have a good hamburger than a steak. I hate wine and all other alcoholic beverages. I smoke cigars, listen to country music and jazz, and go to the movies a lot. We have horses, cats, a dog, and chickens; we grow stuff in our own garden and yes, I even have my very own tractor I use to plow that garden.

So there you have it- the real me. Now let's spend the rest of this book getting to know my students who have taken action and succeeded wealth and on you and how I can add your name to our millionaires club....quickly.

HOW TO GET STARTED AS A REAL ESTATE ENTREPRENEUR

During my travels, one question comes up repeatedly in my conversations with students: "How do I get started?" In our relentless pursuit of the dollar, we sometimes get sidetracked and forget the basics. Each time I've personally lost track of the fundamentals, it has resulted in another expensive seminar at "Idiot School." I don't care how smart you are- or think you are- this business has rules like any other. If you forget the rules, or fail to learn them in the first place, it'll cost you, believe me.

During my career of buying and selling over 2,000 houses, I've made a lot of mistakes. Some were very costly, not only in money but also in needless anxiety. When I look back, I see that most of those screw-ups could have been easily avoided if I had stuck to my own advice.

Yes, I realize this is only a book. You'll read it, toss it aside, and go on about your business. That's OK, but at least read it two or three times before you drop it in the circular file. It just might save you a lot of grief. In my chapter I'll talk about getting started, the basic principles for those who are new to the business and along the way you old pros may pick up some pearls of wisdom from my students. This book is loaded with pearls.

There are three reasons to be in any business:

1. Cash now, in a lump sum

2. Cash flow daily, weekly and monthly

3. Cash in the future

Some people get in the business with the mistaken impression that cash in the future in more important than cash flow now. How many times have you heard of people going one, two or even three years in a startup business before they show a profit?

This kind of foggy thinking keeps the bankruptcy courts full. Only idiots would start a business knowing they would have to endure a negative cash flow for such an extended period of time. I know there are rare exceptions when it may work, but for the sake of this book, I'll assume if you're in the real estate business, your situation is not one of the exceptions. Therefore, if you're operating with a negative cash flow, you've qualified for a seminar in the School of Hard Knocks. If there is one thing I know for certain, it's this: Negative cash flow has no place in life of an intelligent real estate entrepreneur!

So if you're just beginning, concentrate on creating income streams that put money in your pocket, not on business that suck it out. Take care of today's cash flow needs before worrying about building an empire. Focus on cash flow now, growth later. You see, you can't get to the future without first going through the present.

HOW DO YOU KNOW WHERE TO START?

Now it's time to get to the heart of the question. And by the way, don't feel that you're the only person who's ever asked it. Unfortunately, it's hard to pick the right approach when you know very little about any of them. So how can you get this kind of information? You have it in your hands.

It's the beginning of a whole new lifestyle if you use it. The next best thing I would suggest is to make sure, when I or my staff gets anywhere near your area to conduct a seminar that you attend. My seminars have changed thousands of times.

If you'd like introductory, very impressive course on how to capitalize on the bonanza in foreclosures in today's market, go to RonsForeclosureCourse.com. The 90% off offer may still be up when you get there.

Ultimately, the answer of where to start must come from within you. But because there is a way to explore your options with no pain and little cost, I think that way is the wisest course of action. That way is to take a little time to get some basic information on which ideas float your boat. It sure saves a lot of time saddling the wrong horses!

The second step in the plan is to learn the basics. Don't confuse this with learning everything there is to know before doing anything. That's the worst success killer in business. It's called "paralysis of analysis." If you try to get all the answers before you saddle up for the ride, you'll never experience the thrill of the chase. Not only that, but the longer you wait, the harder it gets.

DON'T EXPECT TO BE AN EXPERT BEFORE YOU BEGIN

PERFECTION LEADS TO PARALYSIS!

There are two ways to get an education. The first is at The School of Hard Knocks. The tuition in this school is very expensive and time consuming. In today's environment of readily available information, only a fool would choose this route. It's hard, it's long, it's expensive and it's loaded with death traps that kill dreams and illuminate fortunes. Most people never graduate from this school because the price and sacrifices are just too high.

Those few that have graduated have a lot of stories to tell, but I've never met one of them who didn't wish he or she could've taken and easier route. Yes, there is another route! It's less painful, a lot quicker and cost only a fraction of Hard Knocks University.

Anyone can enroll, regardless of race, creed, sex or financial condition. Graduation comes with fewer scars, and the success rate is many times greater than it is when you take the hard, expensive route. What school am I referring to?

THE UNIVERITY OF PRIOR LEARNING

The only people qualified to teach at this school are those who have gone before you and paved the way in whatever endeavor you choose. Learning from the right teachers is always cheaper, without exception, regardless of what it cost.

The number of people who think it's cheaper to get answers on their own never cease to amaze me! My friend, if there's one important message you get from this book, please let it be this: *The cost of education is always cheaper than is the price of ignorance!*

Regardless of the business you're in, there are always those who have gone before you, willing to teach you what they know. However, it's a big mistake to believe that information of this quality is free. There's an investment to be paid. Just remember this:

FREE ADVICE IS ALMOST ALWAYS WORTH WHAT IT COST,

BUT GOOD ADVICE IS ALMOST NEVER FREE!

I don't say that because I am in the information business and get paid to give good advice. I practice what I preach and will pay handsomely to learn what I don't know, especially if it will help make me money.

Before I continue, I have to clarify one thing. There's a big difference between those who are willing to teach and those who are qualified to teach. It's your responsibility to distinguish between the two; but don't get upset if you choose incorrectly sometimes. There are a lot of phonies who bill themselves as experts. If you mistakenly pay to see one, it's just another part of your education.

At the same time you're learning the business, you'll also learn who's qualified to teach it and who isn't. I'm just suggesting that before you hire a consultant, attend a seminar, or act on financial advice, ask yourself:

TO WHOM ARE YOU LISTENING?

Listening to the wrong people will put you exactly where they want you to be – broke. Learn to separate the wheat from the chaff as you seek out your sources.And...

NEVER TAKE FINANCIAL ADVICE FROM SOMEONE WHO

ISNT MAKING SEVERAL TIMES YOUR INCOME!

Your accountant or your lawyers are probably not competent to teach you how to make money. The average accountant makes $38,000 per year. The average lawyer makes $58,000. Can they teach you to be rich? Obviously, the same question applies to your friends, associates, and your brother-in-law. If they ain't rich, they ain't qualified!

Step three in the plan is to proceed immediately to your first deal. Don't pass go. Don't wait for all the answers. Its far better to do it right away than to do it right.

In fact, you should learn to operate in the real estate business without taking any financial risk at all. That way, any mistakes you make won't be devastating. If you haven't learned a risk free plan yet, start small until you do.

The key is movement, not perfection. Even if your first deal isn't as good as those that made It into my book, it will still be a very important deal in your career. So get on with it, get all the answers as you go, not before you start.

Reading books and listening to tapes are great ways to gain an understanding of something, and that's important. But they cannot teach you how to do it. It takes practice, practice, practice,. Which brings me to one of the most adhered to of all business myths: Practice makes perfect. This is nothing but caca!

ONLY PERFECT PRACTICE MAKES PERFECT!

Doing the same old stupid things every day only makes you older and more frustrated, not richer and wiser. You should be constantly trying to improve your craft. Don't fall into a trap of complacency and get so full of yourself that you quit learning. There's always someone who knows more about your business then you do. If you want to eliminate a lot of years in the ugly school of hard knocks and start your career with same training that that launched every career within this book go to RonsQuickTurn.Com and see how I can help you make a quantum leap.

How many times have you heard people say, "You can't teach me anything; I've been doing this for 20 years!"? Yet when you take a close, hard look, these people don't know much more now than they did 20 years ago! They haven't grown or expanded their knowledge, and the world I passing them by. Anyone who has been doing anything in the business world for 20 years should be filthy rich, or that person is definitely not qualified to be your mentor.

The real trick to getting started fast is learning how to avoid some of the deep potholes you may find in the early part of your journey. Let's examine a few common causes of failure so you'll be able to see them coming and steer clear before they stop you dead in your tracks.

LACK OF MONEY OR CREDIT

Actually, this is not an obstacle. The good thing about the real estate business is that it doesn't take money of credit to get rich. If you don't believe that, I'll introduce you to dozens of students who'll prove it to you in this book. When you begin, concentrate on methods that don't require and cash, at least none of your own. These nothing-down methods require less than a few hundred dollars. Just remember one thing though: When you start making money, don't forget the methods you used to get it and begin doing stupid things that involve foolish risk! Just keep building your empire, conserving capital and avoiding risk.

LACK OF TIME

The question to keep asking is not whether you have time, Instead, ask whether it's worth your time. Every human being alive has the same number of hours in a day as you. Donald Trump, Ted Turner, Bill Gates, and you and I all have the same 24 hours to use in each day. The only thing that separates the super achievers from the masses is what we choose to do with our time. That's it! Like it or not that is the big difference.

This is a fact you can accept, deny, or ignore. Whichever you do, you'll still have to deal with allocating your time to become a super achiever. You have no choice. Ninety-five percent of what we do every day doesn't mean spit. You owe it to yourself and your family to…

FIND OUT WHAT WILL PRODUCE THE MOST INCOME

FOR YOU AND GIVE IT YOUR LASER BEAM FOCUS!

They only way to never fail is to never try. However, true failure and stress come from staying at a job you hate. Unfortunately+, the one pothole that stops more success vehicles than any other is...

FEAR OF FAILURE

It's not a matter of taking a chance. It's a matter of giving yourself a chance. There's nothing wrong with occasional failures as long as you're failing forward. Then you're actually succeeding. No individual success or failure is final. My advice: concentrate on your future success and forget your past failures.

THERE COMES A TIME WHEN YOU MUST TURN AND FACE THE TIGER

Ask yourself, "What have I got to lose?" As Willie Mays used to say, "It's not my life and it's not my wife, so why worry?!" Think about the things you can change and forget those you can't.

There's no way you will ever get rich without failing. You just ain't that good. Neither am I, nor is any human being ever born. Life and business are a never-ending series of mistakes. Any problem solved will be immediately replaced with another, more complicated one. So quit crying over spilled milk and go milk another cow.

WEALTH COMES FROM CHAOS

So go make a big mess! The whole world expects you to fail anyway; why let them down? The difference between you and them is you're failing forward. If you're gonna hang around me, that's the only kind of acceptable failure. Just keep floundering and failing until you're so rich it just doesn't matter anymore. It sure beats the alternative!

THE BEST WAY TO PREDICT YOUR FUTURE IS TO CREATE IT.

If you'd like a skilled Mentor by your side for six months to guide you one on one through your first few deals go to MyMentoringMillionaires.com and meet them. Some have chapters in this book.

ABOUT THIS BOOK

Throughout this book, you'll find real life stories and methods from my students who demonstrate the change that has taken place in their lives. Although this may be unusual way to create a book, I can't think of anything more important for you to read than the success of those who started with nothing but commitment and overcame adversity, some becoming multimillionaires very quickly.

Many thanks to these contributors and may your contribution be in the next edition.

"Deals are my art form. Other people paint beautifully on canvas or write wonderful poetry. I like making deals, preferably big deals. That's how I get my kicks."

Donald Trump

Free CD Order Form
of Ron LeGrand Interviews

As my way of saying thanks for buying this book I'd be pleased to send you any or all of the CD's below, each worth $19.95, a **total value of $79.80** for *only $12.95* S&H. But there's a catch. Not a big catch, just a small favor. All I ask is you tell your friends about my book and maybe a polite nudge to get them to buy.

Check all CD's you'd like to receive. The S&H is the same for one or all.

❏ **How You Can Be A Quick Turn Real Estate Millionaire Without Previous Experience**
This frank discussion with Mentor Magazine explores the lucrative world of quick turn real estate and where the really big money is made including behind the scenes secrets rarely disclosed elsewhere.

❏ **Everything You Ever Wanted To Know About Land Trusts**
This interview answers every question ever asked about how, why and when to use land trusts to buy real estate and discusses the risks you take if you don't.

❏ **How To Bomb Proof Your Assets**
This interview with a national attorney who specializes in asset protection, estate planning, tax reduction and entity structuring could save you a fortune and be the difference between keeping or losing a lifetime of wealth.

❏ **Where To Get The Money**
This interview explains where you can get all the money you'll need to buy and rehab properties regardless of your credit or financial condition. It contains the secrets banks don't want you to know and Ron explains how he got started with no money or credit and overcame bankruptcy to buy over 40 houses his first year.

Free CD Order Form
of Ron LeGrand Interviews

Please Print Clearly

Name: _____

Address: _____

City: _____ State: _____

Zip: _____

Phone: (____) _____ Cell: (____) _____

Fax: (____) _____

Email: _____

Check Only One

<u>Credit or Debit Card:</u>

☐ Please charge credit card _____, exp. date _____

$12.95 for S&H.

<u>ACH Payment or Bank Draft:</u>

☐ Routing Number _____

Account Number _____

Authorized Signature _____

(Must have the information above. No P.O. Boxes please. S&H covers all CDs selected.)

1) *Order* online at **http://www.RonLeGrand.com/4FreeCDs**
2) *Fax* this completed order form to: **888-840-8385 or 904-262-1464** (24 hours/7 days a week)
3) *Mail* this completed order form with check to:
   Global Publishing, Inc. 9799 St. Augustine Road Jacksonville, FL 32257
4) *Call:* **1-888-843-8389 (M-F 9am ET-5pm ET)**

Would you like to be a ☐ Full Time or ☐ Part Time investor?

What would you expect to make your first year?

_____

What would stop you?

_____

When would you like to start?

_____

CHAPTER 1

THE WHO, WHAT, WHERE, WHEN, WHY & HOW OF REAL ESTATE INVESTING

by Brian T. Evans Jr.

Do you ever feel like you are working too hard for your living, and not getting ahead fast enough? Perhaps everything you are doing feels like you are moving one step forward and two steps back.

Do you ever feel like you're missing something and that something must be slipping through the cracks and keeping you from reaching your full potential? Whatever your particular situation, there are millionaire secrets and tricks of the trade that I will share with you, to help you move faster along that proverbial learning curve and to reach greater levels of success.

If you would love to find a single, all-under-one-roof, one-stop-shop source of legitimate, tested, proven, yet original, innovative, even radical strategies for making huge money, growing massive wealth, and rapidly launching your real estate investing career, then this cutting edge information is for you.

If you're reading this book today then you are probably someone who has an interest in becoming a real estate investor or growing your already existing real estate investing business, and for that I congratulate you.

If you've been a past victim of "buy my course and you'll make millions overnight" then don't blame yourself because it isn't your fault. The truth is real estate investing isn't for everyone, and that's ok. It's taken me years to become a success and as a result I've discovered, and now I teach, "real estate investing isn't a get-rich-quick business, but it is a get-rich-quicker-than-other-businesses business, when done right."

I want you to know that a committed and self-made millionaire investor has written this chapter for you - in an attempt to open your eyes and inspire you about the real income potential of this business. In fact, I would wager that you and I are not all that different. I was once a flat-broke country boy from Kentucky who took the bus to work everyday, struggled to pay my bills, had growing credit card debt, and no money in the bank.

I recall one year in my past-life when things couldn't look any worse. I read a book (similar to this one) about the power and potential of real estate investing. It completely transformed my mind and gave me enough motivation to want to learn more. As a result, I've never looked back since. I am now a millionaire real estate investor, author, speaker and mentor, and this was all achieved by the age of 28. I am the founder of an elite network of real estate entrepreneurs called Ultimate Real Estate Investors:

www.UltimateRealEstateInvestors.com

I still invest in real estate full time, doing around 2-6 houses per month, with over 25 deals working at any given time, and a complete resume of deals totaling in the hundreds. My wife and I now live in a gorgeous 25 acre million dollar estate in Lexington, which backs up to the Kentucky River.

I share this little bit of personal history with you to give you hope and to prove to you that if a 'broke' country boy from Kentucky can start at the bottom and find a way to the top, then so can you. You just have to want it bad enough! So, if you would love to gain millionaire status as a real estate investor by increasing your income and decreasing your stress, then keep reading. I've segmented this chapter into six very simple sections in an attempt to prove to you that you can make millions, grow wealth, and retire young with real estate.

WHO IS REAL ESTATE INVESTING FOR?

Real estate investing is for:

1. The small business owner who is "working too hard to make a living" or always worrying about where the next customers are coming from.

2. Owners, Presidents, executives of mid-sized companies frustrated with slow growth, tough and "cheap price" competition, wondering where your next big business breakthrough might come from.

3. Men and women stuck in unfulfilling jobs, eager to own their own businesses, to find new opportunities, to go from "9 To 5" to "MY OWN BOSS," to do something interesting and exciting.

4. Sales professionals struggling to gain ground... weary of "cold" prospecting, tired of fighting just to get an opportunity to sell, thinking there must be a better way.

5. E-Commerce and Internet savvy people with the ambition to use their knowledge for profit.

6. Even authors, speakers, coaches and consultants will be "blown away" by the opportunities and strategies - by the whole world they didn't know existed, its doors thrown open wide with real estate.

7. And ANYONE who simply wants to get more done, to make more money, grow massive wealth, to act with greater confidence, to think more creatively; even to be healthier and more in control of their life and future.

WHAT IS REAL ESTATE INVESTING?

Before I tell you what real estate investing is, I first want to tell you what it is not. Good news, it's not rocket science, or a business that requires a 6th sense. Nor does it require money, credit, or previous experience to achieve millionaire success.

Instead, this business is nothing more than simple math and a simple system. I don't care whether you are a seasoned investor or a 'just off the boat' investor, you CAN make serious money in this business if you apply yourself.

Here's the simple math part of the business. Think about it like this, if you buy a widget for $10.00 and you sell it for $15.00 then you made five bucks. The only difference with real estate is that you add a few more zeros. Therefore, if you buy a house for $100,000 and sell it for $150,000 then you made $50,000! Ok, I know that number is difficult for some people to comprehend so lets just say that you sell the same house for $115,000 and you make $15,000. How many of those deals do you need to do in a month to surpass your current income?

Here's the simple system part of the business. There are 5 steps to success as a real estate investor and if you sway from any of these five steps you will NOT succeed. However if you follow these 5 steps that I am about to share with you, no matter what type of deal you pursue then you WILL succeed, it is only a matter of time.

The 5 Steps to Ultimate Success when BUYING HOUSES:
Step #1: Locate Sellers
Step #2: Prescreen Sellers
Step #3: Construct and Present Offers to Sellers
Step #4: Follow up and Get a Commitment from Sellers
Step #5: Close Quickly and Repeat

The 5 Steps to Ultimate Success when SELLING HOUSES:
Step #1: Locate Buyers
Step #2: Prescreen Buyers
Step #3: Construct and Present Offers to Buyers
Step #4: Follow up and Get a Commitment from Buyers
Step #5: Close Quickly and Repeat

Notice any similarities between the steps to follow when buying houses and selling houses? That's right, the process is exactly the same on the front end as on the back end.

In my office we follow these same 5 steps EVERYDAY when buying and selling properties and we have over 25 deals happening at any given time. Yes, there are some nuances within each of these five steps, but what I'm giving you now is 'The Big Picture.'

Every successful business in the world has systems and steps that are followed day-in and day-out. A business can't run without a system and step-by-step processes. Correction, a PROFITABLE business can't run without a system and step-by-step processes.

If something doesn't seem to be working properly within your business then take a step back, look at 'The Big Picture', review these five steps and find out where within these steps the problem is occurring. I guarantee it will fall within one of them.

So whatever you do, don't complicate this business or try to invalidate what I say because I do it everyday and these are the facts. Just remember, when you follow the system and you sell a house for more than what you bought it for, you make money! The better you get at buying, the easier it will be for you to sell and the more money you'll make.

WHERE DOES REAL ESTATE INVESTING WORK?

Real estate investing works wherever there are houses and wherever there are people. That's right, it works everywhere. I believe it is best to invest in an area you are familiar with such as your local market. The more familiar you are with your local market the more successful you'll be and the more confident you'll be in the investment decisions that you make. This doesn't mean that you have to be an expert and know every little detail about your area, but it does mean that you should have a strong understanding of it. With a strong general knowledge you'll be able to best determine whether you want to hold a property or flip a property based on the various area conditions in your market.

I would recommend devoting a few hours out of your day once this week toward developing a strong understanding of the market you are investing in. Some of the statistics I would recommend you look for are:

- Population
- Area's growth rate
- Area's median income
- Areas education level
- What are the primary industries?
- Is the market growing or shrinking?
- Where are the high-end properties?
- Where are the low-end properties?
- Where are the jobs located?
- Where are the best shopping and entertainment centers?
- Which areas are suffering from high turnover?

- Are new transportation corridors in the offing?
- What are the absorption rates for commercial and residential areas?
- Where is the overall national economy on its gravitational cycle?
- What effect is the current global market having on jobs, land and the overall economy?
- How does the area compare, statistically, to other areas of similar size?

Market info is available from the US census bureau, chambers of commerce, real estate professionals, banks and lenders, tax rolls, industry publications, online websites, etc.

WHEN IS THE BEST TIME TO INVEST IN REAL ESTATE?

It seems like you can't open a newspaper these days without reading something about the financial problems people are having with real estate, unemployment, the economy, foreclosures, bankruptcy, etc. The good news is that it truly doesn't matter what the economy is doing. When you invest the right way, and set yourself and your business up to be a transaction engineer then you can make money and grow wealth when times are both good or bad, and this really is the only way you should approach this business.

A better question for you to consider is this. When would NOW be a good time to start making your millions investing in real estate?

WHY SHOULD YOU INVEST IN REAL ESTATE?

I came up with a phrase years ago that I repeat to myself many times during a given day or week. That phrase is... *"Do Your Best and Let God Do The Rest."* This little saying is extremely powerful and re-assuring to me. When I say it to myself it gives me confidence and strength during times when I feel stressed and weak. You see, we all face difficult decisions, and go through challenging times on a regular basis. It doesn't matter if you are black, white, red, or yellow. It doesn't matter if you have $100 in your bank account or $1,000,000. We all put our pants on one leg at a time, we all enjoy a good dinner and a movie, we all go to bed at night and wake up to the same sun the next day. We are all basically the same.

What makes me different and keeps me going personally in business and life, during times when 99.99% of others would "give up," is my inner drive to *do my best and reach for the stars every single day.* You see, I believe that as long as I do my best and everything in my power to do my best, be positive and a good person, and work hard to grow my business financially, then God will do the rest!

You may be thinking to yourself …why should you consider taking the time to be a real estate investor when you already have so many other things going on in your life. It's a fair question, and I have a fair answer for you. The reason is because you deserve to finally reap the financial rewards of your daily efforts, and this won't happen if you are stuck in a dead-end job, working 9 to 5, and living month-to-month off your current paycheck.

<u>No matter how much you wish for change, things will always stay the same unless you take action and make an effort to try something new and exciting, like real estate investing.</u>

HOW DO YOU INVEST AND MAKE MONEY IN REAL ESTATE?

Ultimately if you want to be a millionaire real estate investor then you need to become a *transaction engineer*. That means you need to know and apply MULTIPLE ways to buy and sell properties. The more ways that you know how to buy and sell real estate, the more deals you can do, the more money you'll make, the more confident you'll be, the more control you'll have, the more freedom you'll have, and the more secure your life will be.

Below are the primary ways to get rich in real estate, however each bullet below can literally be seen as an individual business model all by itself. In fact, I could create dozens of different buying and selling scenarios with each model.

<u>Buying Houses:</u>

- Buy for cash at a discount - Your cash/credit, partner's cash/credit, private lender, hard money lender

19

- Take over debt - Otherwise referred to as buying "subject to." Subject to the existing mortgage(s) on the property. The ownership transfers to you, but the mortgage stays in the seller's name.
- Buy with seller financing - Get ownership of a property and ask the seller to agree to a 'carry-back' note and mortgage on the home.
- Buy on a Short Sale - Working with a seller who is behind in mortgage payments and negotiating with the lender in an attempt to create a discounted mortgage payoff.
- Buy wholesale from other investors - Your cash/credit, partner's cash/credit, private lender, hard money lender
- Buy or create real estate paper assets - Often times the paper on the real estate can be more valuable to you as the investor if you know how to control or discount it.
- Buy on a Lease Option - Instead of actually buying a home you could potentially lease the home from a seller with the right to buy it.
- Buy using your Self-Directed Roth IRA – and get tax-free profits for life!

Selling Houses:

- Retail the property - Fixing up a home and selling to an end user/owner occupant buyer who will cash you out.
- Wholesale a property - Selling a property that you have under contract to another investor who's intent is to rehab and retail the property.
- Assign a contract - Alternative to wholesaling, you can simply assign a contract to purchase to another investor buyer and avoid closing on a property altogether.
- Lease Option/Rent To Own - Collect a non-refundable option deposit from a tenant buyer and give them the right to buy the home and cash you out at a future date.
- Monthly cash flow from the monthly payment of your tenant buyer.
- Cash out money when/if your tenant buyer exercises the option to buy.
- Sell with seller financing - Sell to a new buyer and you 'carry

back' a note and mortgage on a home. May also be referred to as selling on a Land Contract or Contract for Deed, or All Inclusive Trust Deed.

- Sell doing a 'Round Robin' Auction - Intent is to market a property very heavily and in a short period of time to quickly find a 'cash-out' buyer over the period of one weekend.
- Sell your seller carry back note - If you sell using seller financing you can sell the note at a discount to a note buyer and 'cash-out.'

<u>Other Income Streams:</u>

- Sell Leads – Did you know that the buyer and seller leads that you generate with your marketing can be worth something to other people? The key is finding people willing to pay you for your information.
- Down Payment Assistant Program - Collect additional down payment money from your tenant buyers over and above their lease payment each month and apply it to their down payment. This money is also non-refundable.
- Discount 'carry back' notes prior to 'cash-outs' - If you buy on seller financing, you could always request a discount on the note if you pay off early.
- Seller pays you to buy their home - Sound crazy? Perhaps, but you'd be surprised. Some sellers desperate enough will offer to pay you to buy their house.
- Find Deals and Bring to a Partner to Complete - Perhaps you are timid or are still unsure how to do some deals. Simply bring them to someone who knows how to do them and ask to do a profit split. I do this frequently with some students and everyone wins.

It is impossible for me to teach you everything you need to know about "how-to" invest in real estate in one chapter of a book. However, as I bring this lesson to a close, your choices now are simple.

<u>Option #1:</u> Do nothing today and continue along the same path of one step forward and two steps back. This is obviously the easiest choice because it's the path of least resistance, but it's by far the most costly to your current and future financial success.

<u>Option #2:</u> quit letting thousands of dollars slip away and make a commitment to yourself that you will learn how to get rich with real estate by going to: www.UltimateRealEstateInvestors.com.

It has been a pleasure bringing this important information to you and I wish you the very best of success. You are well on your way to becoming a millionaire real estate investor.

To Your Ultimate Success,

Brian Evans
www.UltimateRealEstateInvestors.com

ABOUT BRIAN

Brian Evans was once a flat-broke country boy from Kentucky, turned Wall Street employee drop out, turned failed retail coffee shop owner, turned real estate investor, turned Millionaire real estate expert, Author, Speaker and Mentor by the age of 28. He still invests in real estate full time doing anywhere from 2-6 houses per month, with over 25 deals working at any given time, and a complete resume of deals totaling in the hundreds. He is now married with kids on the way, lives in a gorgeous 25 acre Million Dollar Estate in Lexington, which backs up to the Kentucky River.

He is the founder of a national real estate investing group called Ultimate Real Estate Investors, whose motto is: Make Money, Live Wealthy, No Excuses. This is the place where leading investors from all over the country come together to achieve exceptional goals, develop lasting relationships, make real money, master the business of real estate investing once and for all, and turn dreams into reality!

Brian teaches and personally invests in all types of real estate from single family homes to multifamily and commercial using creative techniques such as **short sale, seller financing, subject to, option, lease option, wholesaling, retailing, round robin, self directed Roth IRA, private mortgage loans**, etc. He can honestly say that he's started at the bottom and invested his way to the top. "I'm not an exceptional individual," says Brian, "just an individual that chooses to be exceptional."

To learn more about Brian Evans and his real life insider secrets for making huge money, growing massive wealth, and rapidly launching a real estate investing career, go to: www.UltimateRealEstateInvestors.com

For a limited time only, he is giving away: The Most Incredible Free Real Estate Money Making Gift on the Planet, Guaranteed! (Value = $1,620.94). This package (may be subject to change) includes:

Gift #1: 30 Minute 1-on-1 Make Money In Real Estate Jumpstart Conference Call with Brian Evans. (Value = Priceless)

Gift #2: Manual and CD's: "77 Biggest Mistakes Real Estate Investors Make." ($997 Value).

Gift #3: CD-ROM of Brian's 50 Most Commonly Used Real Estate Forms ($387 Value).

Gift #4: Free Membership to "Foreclosure Gold Rush Live" website ($39.95 Value).

Gift #5: Everything you need to Attract Private Lenders ($147 Value).

Gift #6: One-month access to Ultimate Real Estate Investors membership (<u>$49.97 Value</u>).

Includes mailed monthly newsletter and how-to CD of the month. Weekly Q&A conference calls. Deal structuring support, Resources and more! (<u>$49.97 Value</u>).

Gift #7: Six Month Access to "What Would Evans Do" Fax Hotline. (<u>Value = Priceless</u>).

PLUS more surprise money-making goodies that he'll share with you after you take action that will benefit your income tremendously!

You may now consider Brian a part of your support network, and he can be contacted any of the following ways:-

Phone: 1-800-282-4653 Fax: 1-859-201-1441

Email: info@UltimateRealEstateInvestors.com

Website: www.UltimateRealEstateInvestors.com

Address: 3070 Lakecrest Circle 400-260 Lexington, KY 40513

CHAPTER 2
THE TREADMILL: GOOD FOR RUNNING NOWHERE

by Caitie Yue

always wanted to be an entrepreneur. I didn't have a newspaper route or a lemonade stand, but from a fairly early age, I knew I was different: I wanted to be the master of my own destiny. I dreamed of being an owner of a small business, but never imagined I'd be a real estate entrepreneur with a $15 million dollar portfolio at the age of 27.

My parents, refugees and immigrants, came to Canada with nothing more than the clothes on their backs. Their dreams and lives were uprooted by circumstances beyond their control, but they never complained. They worked hard—really hard—for very little. Life wasn't easy, but they built a good home and I had a happy childhood.

They had no illusions of achieving the great Canadian dream though; all they wanted was for their children to take advantage of the opportunities they never had. Education was very important in our family and we were all expected to attend and graduate from university.

I started running on the treadmill called work at the tender age of 14. While my parents did a good job of hiding our true financial picture from us, I still knew there was no secret education account to fund the future tuition fees and I wanted to come up with the funds myself. By chance, I saw a part-time cashier position posted in the window of the local drugstore and decided to apply. I had never interviewed for a job before and didn't even have a social insurance number, but managed to land the job. I worked at that drugstore for almost a decade, through high school, university and two full-time jobs. To this day I am grateful to the manager who took a chance on the kid who didn't know any better and wore overalls to her interview. Because of her, I managed to graduate from university with no debt.

I thought I was ahead. No debt! University graduate! Bright future ahead! I was earning more money than my parents and able to take vacations and go out for dinners. But reality soon set in and I realized I was just running on a treadmill, going nowhere. So I did what I thought made sense: I found another job. I worked for a start-up as a graphics designer. I was excited; my co-workers were young and hungry and I felt like I was a part of a real team. It was a different world than my previous job in publishing. We all worked long hours, but we felt like we were contributing to something big. My dreams of being a small business owner were put on the backburner. Seduced by benefits and stock options, the bi-weekly paycheck was the kind of stability that made my parents proud.

My parents believed that you made money by putting money in the bank. They may have been risk takers with their personal lives, but they were not risk takers when it came to finances. They believed success in life depended on how much money you could save and viewed debt as a bad thing, whether it was mortgage or credit card debt. Their motto was "Go to work, work hard, and the money will come." Even though I knew there was something missing from this way of thinking, I couldn't figure out how to escape the rat race.

My life changed in 2003 when I met my now-husband, Jason. He is everything I'm not: logical, calm and analytical. We discovered our mutual love of learning and he encouraged me to dream even bigger dreams. He nurtured my love of business and taught me more about finance and investing. We attended financial seminars and investing expos, read 'tons' of books and 'hatched' business plans. We contemplated franchising, Internet businesses and even reselling popular items on eBay. But none of these ideas spelled real financial freedom, so we kept learning and reading. Then we noticed a trend among many of the authors whose books we were reading: they had made their fortunes in real estate.

After many months of debate, discussion and research, we finally decided to take the plunge and invest in real estate. We interviewed realtors and finally found one who understood our criteria and our goals. We had strict criteria and wanted healthy cash flow – the rent had to cover the mortgage, insurance, taxes, management fees and then some. Our strategy was to buy properties for long-term holding and we didn't want to depend solely on capital appreciation for gains. It was disheartening at times. We viewed dozens and dozens of properties until finally, in 2006, we purchased our first investment property in a small town north of Toronto. It was a lovely detached home in a good neighborhood that we planned to convert to a home with a legal basement suite. We were terrified. Neither one of us knew anything about renovations but tackled the challenge head-on, making mistakes as we went along but learning every step of the way.

The project look much longer than expected and I was constantly on the phone with angry neighbors, the town council, contractors, inspectors and prospective tenants. We had read books and joined an investment network but nothing prepared us for the real thing. It was scary and thrilling at the same time.

By the end of that first year, we had purchased a total of five properties and were hungry for more. Our initial plan was to purchase a few investment properties to diversify our investment portfolio, but the more I immersed myself in the world of real estate, the more I loved it. I was working 18-hour days between my day job and real estate, not going to bed until after midnight every night. Every spare moment I had was spent searching for deals, looking at properties, analyzing properties, or screening new tenants. Even though it was time-consuming and left little time for much else, we both loved it and couldn't get enough.

In December 2006, Jason tried to convince me to quit my job and become a full-time real estate entrepreneur. I didn't want to give up the security blanket I had and resisted. I'm not kidding you - my list of fears and excuses was two pages long. My "what ifs" list was even longer. I didn't want to let down my team at my job, I was worried about money and I was afraid of failing. For weeks, I debated the pros and cons and had many sleepless nights. I let my fears take control and almost decided not to quit until Jason helped me realize that I was looking at it the wrong way. I wasn't letting anyone down except myself if I didn't at least try. So we mapped out a plan of acquiring another 15 properties that year and researched other cities in other provinces and started making calls to the different contacts we had networked with throughout our year of investing. It took me a month to mentally prepare myself to even write my letter of resignation but when I finally did, I knew I had made the right decision.

In April 2007, I quit. I think almost everyone I knew thought I was crazy, especially my parents. I had a good job at a great company where I had plenty of room to grow; I had regular paychecks and my bi-annual visits to the dentist were covered; even I was convinced I had 'lost my marbles.' But I was determined to succeed, and failure was not an option I allowed myself to think of.

Two days after my last official work day, we headed west to Alberta, the land of oil and opportunity. The real estate market was hot but the fundamentals were there. Jobs, growth, and great government support were just a few signs that it wasn't just smoke and mirrors. We did our homework and researched different cities and areas until finally settling on a smaller city in central Alberta. Then we started buying… and buying and buying and buying. We even bought while we were on vacation in Eastern Europe, using ancient fax machines with thermal paper in remote towns of the Czech Republic.

The next five months were a blur. We were raising investment capital from family and friends and buying properties across the country that fit our criteria. We had meetings with bankers and brokers, agents and investors, lawyers and accountants, property managers and tenants. Life was crazy and hectic but we were having a blast. By August 2007, we had acquired an additional 30 properties, twice our goal in just a few short months. The next year we added another five properties, bringing our total to just over 40 properties.

We still own all those properties except one, the very first property we bought. We sold it in 2008 after one too many tenant headaches. It was a very difficult decision. Our strategy was long-term buy and hold, not flipping or short sales. When it was fully rented, the cash flow was over

$500 a month — what were we, crazy? But it was difficult to manage and I was tired of hearing about squabbling tenants, so we put it on the market and sold it. After commissions and taxes, penalties and renovation costs, our profit came out to zero dollars over the two years we owned it. I'd be lying if I told you I was happy about making no profit, but it was the best zero dollars I've ever made. What we learned during the process was invaluable and we couldn't have paid to learn the lessons we did.

Fast-forward to 2010: Life is still hectic and busy, but I am still loving every minute of it. I know we have planned well for the long-term and have set ourselves up to be financially free in the future with our real estate portfolio. We still continue to look for more investing opportunities, mainly in commercial real estate and building/development but we are taking our time and learning as much as we can. Real estate has changed my life, but it's not just about the money. Real estate has given me a kind of freedom I never thought possible.

KEYS TO SUCCESS:

1. Educate yourself.

Read books, magazines, newspapers and anything else you can to learn as much as you can about real estate.

2. Do your homework.

Before investing in a property, do your homework. Check newspapers for actual rental rates in your area. Crunch the numbers. Don't forget that real estate is not global, national or even city-focused. Real estate statistics are good guidelines but you must do further research to identify anomalies. Contact local town or city council to get a feel for how they view investors and ask for economic data.

3. Build a great team.

From your realtor to your tenant, building a great team is crucial to success. We are eternally grateful to our team for helping us get this far. Our team consists of lawyers, accountants, realtors, property managers, mortgage brokers, bankers and inspectors, as well as an assistant and bookkeeper. They all understand our goals and work with us to achieve them. Don't forget your tenants! Many people think the property is the asset: wrong! Tenants are your assets. Think about it: they essentially pay your mortgage, taxes, insurance, management fees and more, take care of your property, and when they leave, it's still yours.

4. Treat it like a real business.

Whether you are investing in your first property or planning to pursue it full-time one day, run it like a small business. Even if you plan to manage the property yourself, or complete your own renovations, you must account for these expenses in your numbers. I know many investors who've been burned because they didn't treat it like a real business.

5. Make no excuses.

No matter who you are or where you've come from, there is no better time to get started. There is no such thing as perfect timing, and it doesn't matter what your age, sex or level of experience is.

6. Word hard.

There will be days you feel like you're just spinning your wheels, and there will be long, frustrating days where you feel like you want to quit. Keep at it and do that extra 10% others aren't willing to do.

7. Systemize.

Systems are extremely important. From your buying system to your tenant management system, systemizing will help make things easier. If this is not your strength, find someone who is good at it for your team.

8. Surround yourself with the right people.

Ignore the nay-sayers (because there will be many) and surround yourself with like-minded people. Network and find a mentor. The right people will support you, cheer you on, and offer invaluable advice when you need it. Don't be afraid to ask for help from others — you'll be pleasantly surprised at how willing people are to help out fellow investors.

9. Focus on a niche.

You will get distracted by lots of "shiny" things. Try to focus on a specific neighborhood or area, type of home and even type of investing.

10. Cash flow is king.

Every single property we own has a healthy monthly cash flow. When we purchased the properties, we made sure that the monthly rent could cover all of our expenses and were unwilling to accept long-term capital appreciation as the only upside in our investments. This has been crucial to our success at weathering the global economic crisis.

ABOUT CAITIE

Caitie Yue is a Canadian real estate entrepreneur and investor who has invested in residential real estate across Canada. She has helped investors diversify their portfolios through real estate investments with a strong emphasis on long-term growth and cash flow and is the managing director and partner of a portfolio of properties valued at fifteen million dollars.

Caitie is also the co-founder and CEO of Blueprint EQ Developments and Blueprint EQ Capital. She is responsible for building relationships with developers, builders and lenders with a mission to identify and provide exceptional investment opportunities for partners.

Caitie left her job as a graphics designer at a 'hot' start-up company in 2007 to pursue her entrepreneurship dreams and hasn't looked back. She is passionate about promoting financial literacy and entrepreneurship among children and young adults and hopes to inspire a new generation of entrepreneurs.

Caitie lives in Toronto with her husband and continues to learn, explore and invest in high-growth and long-term investment opportunities.

Follow Caitie on Twitter: c8itie

CHAPTER 3
THE YELLOW LETTER

by Donna and John MacNeil

What an honor to be included in the Guru's new book. Thank you Ron!

Real Estate Investing is a great business. Rewarding to all the people involved: you, the seller, the buyer, the contractor, the neighborhood, the private money lenders, the closing attorney, and all the way to the tax rolls.

Investing can have it's ups and downs, but the ups are much much higher than the downs.

Ron once told me if you're not buying and selling enough houses, fix the problem. First you have to find the problem. No, it's not on the computer, not on the CD's or courses.

> *How to find the problem: "Look in the mirror."*
> *How to the fix the problem: "Get to Work!"*

We can only tell you from our own experience that 'getting to work' means getting your marketing up and running. So, we started to mail The **Yellow Letter**! It's a numbers game; the more **Yellow Letters** mailed out... the more the responses, the more incoming calls, the more appointments, the more deals you get, and the more "Money" you make.

Direct mail can be an extremely effective way to find motivated sellers and buy houses and become wealthy, if you know how to do it. As you probably know, most people open their mail over the wastebasket. No message, no matter how effective, is going to generate a response unless your letter gets opened!

Then you have to have a message that will inspire the recipient to take action and call you. With that many potential sellers calling you, you can take your pick of the best deals. The homes with the most equity, best profit, and the quickest cash out. You won't have to waste your time with non-motivated sellers, tire-kickers or time wasters just because you have no one better to work with.

Donna & John's **Yellow Letter** real estate investor marketing system is so simple, an average high school student could do it. You don't have to be a direct mail guru.

What are you waiting for? You town is filled with people waiting to sell you their house. They just need to hear from you. This system will show you how to find motivated sellers in your market! Don't waste your time with marketing that drains your budget and doesn't bring you deals on a regular basis. Try John and Donna MacNeil's real estate marketing letter today! Let me tell you how our Real Estate Investing Business began. After Donna starting working for Ron, she got very interested in the business, meeting with some of Ron's students who became trainers and speakers.

In the mean time my J.O.B. was just fine, good money, pay bonuses, company car, golf outings, etc. Well, deep down I knew the energy industry was headed into trouble with "Enron" and "BP."

As I drove on my daily business, I listened to Sport Talk Shows, until one day an announcer didn't know that Ted Williams the greatest hitter of all time, served with the Marines as a pilot in two wars. I'm a diehard Yankee fan and even I knew that about Ted Williams.

So off went the car radio. In the mean time, Ron had given Donna some old tape, odds and ends of courses, and seminars which she passed onto me. After listening to a few of these tapes I told Donna, "I think we can do this business. Donna set up an appointment with Ron and he spent some time with us. Ron laid out a schedule of events and seminars, much like today's Master Program, and yes, we paid full price. If we had waited 1 year we could have paid 50% less and if we waited two years we wouldn't have to pay at all.

Notice I didn't say save money, because 'waiting' to become successful and rich doesn't work.

SUMMARY

The cost of our training: Priceless.
The return on our training investment: Incalculable!

I started out calling 'For Sale By Owners' in the paper and became an 'ant' for Ron. I'm not a math genius, but a few dollars as an ant is a lot less than wholesaling or retailing a house. So our business began.

Why did I create the **Yellow Letter**? Nothing else worked to our satisfaction. Form letters got a very low response rate. Letters that give sellers false hope, such as "I can save your credit," "I'll stop your foreclosure," and "I'll protect you from bankruptcy"... Bull! Bull! Bull!

Does anyone read a form letter at all? I used postcards but you need a ton of them to get one response. No wonder people try to sell tracking systems to track tons of postcards. Why not use a scale. Postcards are the most expensive way to mail. One card is cheap, but you need tons and tons of them... and the cost adds up.

One national trainer told me he only uses postcards to find empty houses.

Signs, I love signs. Until one day Donna and I spent the morning putting out signs. I jumped in and out of our van as she drove. Three hours later we finished and went to lunch, proud of all our work. After lunch we drove back over the same route where we had placed our signs. Where did they go? We only found three left. The sign police had won. Thank goodness we didn't get any fines.

Well back to the drawing board to start a New Marketing System that would work. I thought back to the home heating oil business I was in. I took a letter and copied a note I had used back in the day, and then turned it into **My Yellow Letter**. We keep revamping the note until we were getting a 35% to 45% response rate on regular basis. It took us about 9 months, but that's what it takes sometimes... and IT WORKED!!!

Since the mortgage and housing change began in 2007, many mail fulfillment companies have failed due to unsound and unstable business practices. Some mail fulfillment companies are just bad apples.

We are **Yellow Letter.com,** you can have confidence in us and here's why.

We're the Original, the first! We created the **Yellow Letter**, and we invented the system that works. We didn't take the idea from someone else or steal their ideas and dreams. We didn't copycat, we didn't need to, we started it!!! When you run your company with integrity and take care of your customers you stay #1.

And we thank you very much.

We're also rated #1 – 5 stars by the country's leading mail analysts, national and international speakers, and Guru's. All have rated us excellent based on our performance and customer satisfaction. Our ratio of 30% response rate still stands. You won't find our name on any complaint lists! We just won't fail you like other mail houses.

Foreclosure rates are at an all time national high and other mailing houses are struggling with lead lists that just aren't working. **Yellow Letter.com**'s exclusive Mail List performs 'way above' the national average. While other mail houses have little regard for their customers, **Yellow Letter.com** works closely with our customers to insure the best results possible.

You can be confident that our goal is to keep our customers happy.

We're a small company by choice. Since 2002 our company has maintained our focus on our customers, not the demands of others. Our approach to marketing has seen our company grow as we continue to guide our customers and watch their success.

We retain 99% of the customers and friends we make. We don't send our customer's names and email addresses to other companies. Also we never sell a customer list to anyone else. Your list is exclusive.

We help our customers manage their lists and mailings and maintain their relationship for the long term. Why does retaining our customer base matter? Our customers always know who to call when they have questions about their lists and mail campaigns, or when it's time to reorder their **Yellow Letters** and lists. We are a company that appreciates working with Real Estate Investors.

While other Mail Houses have shut down or scaled back their operations, **Yellow Letter.com**'s customer base is up 78% in 2009. Why? The answer is our incredibly talented and well trained customer friendly staff, headed up by Donna and Susan.

By following our consistent business model, investors have flocked to **Yellow Letter.com**'s sound, stable, accurate and fast service. Many investors sought out our company after hearing about us through word-of-mouth, a company they could count on. We never lost faith in the American Dream of Home Ownership, the American Dream of Owning your own business. We're proud to service more investors every day that are buying houses across The United States of America and Canada.

THE BOTTOM LINE

We're going strong mailing yellow letters for ten's of thousands of Americans.

How can we Help You?

The current economy has given Real Estate Investors a true advantage, buying and selling houses. This is one of the best times to be in the business of Real Estate Investing, mortgage interest rates are at historic lows. It's a Buyers market; there are plenty of incentives that make Investing more affordable than ever.

<u>**Yellow Letter.com** will put you in front of all the sellers and buyers you need</u>.

Rethink your current marketing. If your response rate is low and your return rate is High, you should consider a fix. It's time to turn that Marketing around. It might be beneficial to contact **Yellow Letter.com** or Email: susang@yellowletter.com or just call Susan at 904-396-0205.

The choice is yours. Consolidate your marketing into a system that produces results and is proven to work. There is no obligation, no fees, and no contracts, unlike some other direct mail programs. We won't charge you hundreds of dollars just to apply.

Marketing is the key to your Real Estate Investing Engine. So start your engine now. The **Yellow Letter** has been voted the #1 Best Marketing Tool in North America, used both in the United States and Canada.

Yellow Letter.com comes in first every time. While copycats and phonies fall by the wayside, John's **Original Yellow Letter** still out produces all the others 10 to 1. **Yellowletter.com** is not affiliated with any of the copycat companies, nor do we endorse any of the phony yellow letter companies. We know that to get the best results with your mail marketing, you must go to: www.yellowletter.com or email: donna@ yellowletter.com or: susang@yellowletter.com

Better yet, _**just call Susan at 904-396-0205**_. Susan is our expert on mailing yellow letters and lists. Susan and her husband Donald help us help you. Donald and Susan have been our dear friends for over 30 years. We know you'll like them too.

I've tried to end this chapter three times. I keep coming up with things I love about this business, our life style and income.

It all started when Donna was the Senior Person in charge of marketing and advertising, working under the Vice President of sales for a local and well known home improvement company. After a failed coup by the Vice President, the owner closed the division. (By the way, that company is no longer in business.)

Donna went to the classified ads in our local paper, a small ad caught her eye "Executive Assistant Wanted." After an interview with Ron Who? "We never heard of this guy." I asked Donna what does he do? "He says he makes people rich" she replied.

Well, he does and we're proud of that today (ten years later). Ron and Bev are some of our closest friends and Ron is still my mentor.

Ron once told me he didn't make me rich, I did. But Ron you sure helped. We couldn't have done it without his advice, training, events, seminars and mentoring.

My Mother thanks you, my wife thanks you, my kids and grandkids thank you and most of all, I Thank You!

Ron never stops making peoples dreams come true. Donna and I know this is true every day as we look over the White River, with our Bald Eagle nest by the river in our Dream Home.

ABOUT DONNA AND JOHN

Donna's professional background in the real estate industry includes being a Realtor for 10 years in New Jersey and also doing appraising for the State in 13 counties. John also dabbled in real estate as an agent, and since partnering with Donna and then starting Family Home Solutions, John has been in the Real Estate Investment trenches... buying and selling houses every day.

John's development of the phenomenal marketing tool, "The Yellow Letter," has added to the list of what investors need - to get their businesses up and running as quickly as possible - with phenomenal marketing.

CHAPTER 4
SEVEN ESSENTIALS TO MAKING MILLIONS WITH REOS

by Eddie Miller

I n the fall of 2008 when the US economy shifted, so did my entire life. I was a project manager for one of the largest commercial interior construction companies in Miami. Almost instantly, construction came to a standstill, and I was left without a job.

Late one night a few months later there was an infomercial for investing in real estate, which led me to researching the top real estate gurus on the internet. The only way to decipher between them all was to pick the one who had the most positive and least negative comments about them, and who had a proven track record. Within two weeks my partner, Alekxey Sabido, and I were sitting in one of Ron LeGrand's training seminars. We left that seminar with a determination to make this business work. However, investing in real estate can be somewhat overwhelming, and one of our first challenges was determining where to start.

From previous experience I knew that if we were going to succeed we had to *focus our intention* by determining what of Ron's training we should really hone in on first, and focus on our intended goals. Once we were clear on our intentions, we had to take action. With Florida being one of the top foreclosure states, we realized our primary focus needed to be on foreclosed REOs—Real Estate Owned by the bank. As a result, we learned to select ideal properties, build a powerhouse team, raise over a million dollars in private funds, and produce great rehabs that sold within days of putting them on the market. In our first year, we made more money than ever before, and became one of the fastest growing private real estate investors in Miami.

1. We've discovered that the *first critical component to our business was to* **"Focus Our Intention and Take Action"** by making offers, talking with potential private lenders, and selling the properties. In this chapter, I'll share exactly how we focused our intention as well as the methods and systems we've created, to 'make a killing' in the REO market.

2. The second essential component was *selecting our properties.*

SELECTING PROPERTIES
THAT MAKE MASSIVE PROFITS

As Ron puts it, "find your bread and butter neighborhoods." You want to identify the neighborhoods in your community that are desirable and where properties are selling—with clean streets and nicely maintained homes. You will find that the prices of the properties will vary depending on where you live.

When selecting your properties, always, always, always follow the **MAO** formula (Maximum Allowable Offer). It's simple, here is how you do it... take the **ARV** (After Repair Value that the house will sell for in 30-60 days) x 70% - Repairs = MAO.

So, if in 30-60 days the house will sell for $100,000, you multiply it by 70% (equaling $70,000), minus repairs, and in this case say they total $20,000, then you know the Maximum Allowable Offer you can make is $50,000. Ideally, we like to use 65% and if possible pay less, but we will never go over 70%. *It is critical to remember if the numbers don't work, **walk away**; there is always another deal out there for you.*

It is also important to note that there may be neighborhoods in your chosen area that the banks may be listing the REOs at or near the ARV. First of all, *make sure your ARV is correct.* If it is, then just put your focused intention on other neighborhoods in your area and periodically keep an eye on the original neighborhood to see if the listing prices change.

In addition, avoid homes that don't have curb appeal, those with odd or unusual interior layouts, and those that are too small. We always ask ourselves "could we live here?" Not that we would, but rather does the house have charm, character, curb appeal, a nice layout, *something* that will help resell it fast.

It typically takes us 8 to 10 offers on average to get a house under contract. So if you want to move fast, have your realtor help you scout out properties from the MLS (Realtors' Multiple Listing Service), search auction websites, and also scout out REO wholesalers—investors who have purchased REOs and resell them with a slight markup.

These wholesalers can typically be found at your local REIA (Real Estate Investment Association) meetings. When you become good at it, you will beat them at their own game and get the properties first, but if you're just starting out this is another good place to begin. We've also purchased several properties from auctions; just make sure to preview the properties prior to the auction day to know your MAO. The internet is a great source to find the auctions in your area. However, when it comes to REO's, we've found the best place is through the MLS, (not REO and foreclosure websites as we found it to be too time consuming); your realtor can automatically set you up for minute-by-minute emails with the latest properties on the market.

Again, the most important thing to remember when selecting properties is the deal has to work with the MAO formula or you walk away. If the numbers don't work right now, check the property in a month or two; you might find the bank is more than happy to accept your offer at MAO or well below.

BUILDING YOUR POWERHOUSE TEAM

To 'make a killing' in the REO business you need to *build a powerhouse team*. One of the first important members is your realtor. Once you identify the neighborhoods where you are going to focus, then the next step is finding a *realtor* that:

1. You enjoy working with

2. Really knows the area
3. Understands market trends and investing
4. Is great at pulling comparables, and
5. Is committed to working with only one investor, at least in your targeted area, so he/she is sending all of the deals your way.

We were extremely fortunate as our realtor, Alice Kellogg, was an amazing goldmine of information and she really helped us learn the ropes. Alice immediately got the MAO formula we used to evaluate properties and continues to always have our best interests in mind. Based on this relationship, we are very loyal to her and only buy and sell properties in her market through her.

Miami is a large city, so as we've expanded to areas outside of Alice's market, we needed to add an additional realtor for each of the areas we've expanded, but each time we expanded we used the same criteria above.

An *REO agent* is a great type of a realtor to seek out. They usually work with several banks and are alerted first of new properties coming on the market. In addition, identify contacts at *small banks and credit unions* in your areas as they could easily provide you first crack at the properties they are getting ready to liquidate.

You will also want to get to know *members of your local REIA group*. It only takes one person to open amazing doors. Usually, they are happy to refer contractors, real estate attorneys, title companies, other investors, etc. in your area to help you build your business. Go to the meetings and find out what's happening and even the great deals in your community.

Your *real estate attorney, title company, and accountant* are also essential, but don't think you have to have them or any of the team members in place beforehand. I'm suggesting you do your first deal first. Start making offers and the right people will fall into place. Once your business starts rocking, you'll soon discover you can't do it all, and as soon as your budget allows, you will need to bring on some help. Today we have a *virtual assistant, acquisitionist, and rehab manager*. [For a list of their job descriptions visit http://www.NewMastersOfRealEstate.com]

Before I go any further… I want to say it again, know you can do your first handful of deals on your own—we did, but eventually you will need support, unless you are only going to buy and sell a few properties a year. The first person I'd add is a virtual assistant who can handle a variety of tasks remotely; jobs like internet research, tracking auctions, uploading properties on your website, placing internet ads, overseeing your social media sites, and answering all phone calls from buyers and realtors to provide showing instructions — the list is endless of what they can do.

In addition, it's great to have an acquisitionist to preview all of the properties. A key to the REO business is acting fast, so as you grow your business you'll find you can't be everywhere at once. Each day, from various sources, you'll get updates of new properties on the market from the MLS and upcoming auctions. It could be 1, 3, or more.

First, have the acquisitionist pull the sold comparable properties (preferably from the last 30-60 days) to determine what price range houses in the neighborhood are selling. If it appears that this is a possible deal, then the acquisitionist will: (a) contact the realtor to preview the property, (b) estimate repair costs using our *Rehab Budget & Checklist*, (c) take photos of the house — especially of major repairs, (d) run by the comparable properties if necessary, (e) check for code violations and liens with the city/county, and (f) report back.

All of the legwork is done, and all you need to preview are the properties for which you want to make offers. Your job is to *make offers, make offers, and make offers!*

Now it really depends on how you would like to structure your business. If you want to primarily wholesale your REOs, then your acquisitionist and virtual assistant will likely be sufficient. Wholesaling is when you have a property under contract and sell it to another investor with a goal to simultaneously buy and sell the property with a profit of $5,000, $10,000, or possibly $20,000. If you don't sell it by your contract closing date, you will need to pay for the property, and continue marketing in order to sell it after purchasing. Or, walk away and lose your escrow deposit. That's the wholesale business.

However, if you are interested in rehabbing, then eventually you could add a rehab manager, although initially our general contractor was a great help until our business grew to the point that we needed someone full-time.

Here is an overview of the rehab manager's responsibilities once the property is under contract:

1. Inspection Period – orders the inspection and appraisal, double check liens and code violations, and that contractors provide rehab budgets... all to confirm this is a property to purchase.
2. Contract Period – take 'before' photos, prep for permits, contact your attorney and title company, and order vacant house and liability insurances to begin the day you close.
3. Rehab Period – pull permits, transfer utilities, monitor contractors and the budget, order final inspections, ensure all final punch list items are complete, and take 'after' photos.
4. Selling Period – list property with realtor and on the internet, create a flyer, monitor maintenance, and manage the showing and closing process.

An important lesson we've learned is that if the person you've hired for any position is not the right fit, then you need to move on and find one who is. It may not be easy at the moment, but if you don't, your business will suffer in the long run.

A little later, I will discuss *your team of contractors*; however, I want to mention the importance of building a solid relationship with each of them. Treat them with respect and appreciate their work, they'll take more pride in your projects and when you really need them to come through for you, they will.

The key to building a powerhouse team and successful business is that **you** are the one who keeps an eye on the pulse of 'what's going on' and 'where you are going.'

RAISING PRIVATE FUNDS—THE EASY WAY!

So you may be asking yourself, "What am I supposed to be doing?" You are the engine, the visionary. Your job is to replace yourself as quickly as possible, manage those you hire to replace you, continue to focus on the new trends in the real estate market, and raise private funds. Raising private funds is vital to the REO business and in this section *I'm going to share how easy it is to do.*

In the beginning I was like most, afraid to talk with people about investing in real estate. I had no credibility—I was the guy without a job. Then at one of Ron's training sessions, he was reviewing the components of working with private lenders. Well, I took great notes and went back home to create what I now call the *Investment Opportunity One-Sheet*. This document reviews how individuals can get a higher return compared to what they are getting with CDs, annuities, stocks, and other investments; and how they could even invest using a self-directed IRA to get a 100% tax-free return. [Get a free copy at: http://www.NewMastersOfRealEstate.com].

It also explains exactly how the process works, we don't borrow more than 70% of the current after repair market value of the property, and that their investment is secured with a mortgage on the property. Plus, we provide a copy of the appraisal, title insurance, and fire/wind insurance policies to insure the security of their investment. Furthermore, we explain the entire transaction, including drawing up the paperwork, the escrow of their investment, and both closings (buying and selling) are handled by an attorney.

Then, in the next part of the process, Alekxey and I each made a list of people we knew that *might* be interested or *might* know someone who would be interested in investing. I stress **might** because you never know what money people have access to, or who they know. I promise you, if you make a list of 40 to 90 people from all over the world (including your family, friends, business contacts, and those you remotely know), these individuals will easily lead you to $250,000 in three months, and will likely lead you to $1 million or more. I promise! We raised over $1 million in our first year of business, and we had private lenders from the US, Mexico, and Europe. We started with family members and friends; then, as our confidence grew, we began talking with others.

We are ALWAYS adding new contacts to our prospect list from events that we attend—like parties and Chamber of Commerce meetings. And we are ALWAYS sharing with others about our real estate business, how we work with private lenders, and how we provide a higher return safely, securely, and ethically. The key is simply talking with people on a daily basis. Whether in person or on the phone, we simply walk-through the key points on our 'one-sheet', answer their questions, give or e-mail them the one-sheet, and follow-up with them to see if they are interested. If not, we ask for a referral. They might not be ready to invest right now, but they likely know someone who is. It really is as simple as that.

Most times as you're talking with people, the conversation will just flow naturally and you're able to share what you are doing. They get interested and you take it to the next step. You can also use what Ron suggests to initiate a conversation, "Do you have an IRA or any other investments not producing a high return safely?"

It is also critical to follow-up. Here is an example. We were having lunch with a good friend. Not expecting she had any money to invest, I simply mentioned that we were looking for a private lender for a new property we were buying and asked if she knew someone. She said she had a friend that might be interested. I sent an e-mail with the one-sheet for her to forward to her friend. When we followed up, her friend wasn't interested, but she herself had $30,000 to invest. The exact amount we needed for one of our rehab projects. She is now on her second investment with us.

So, how do you face the fear of raising private money?

In the process of writing my latest book — *Living Inside-Out: The Go-To Guide for the Overwhelmed, Overworked & Overcommitted*, I discovered that behind 'what we fear the most' is enormous power for us, if we are only willing to 'lean into our fear.' When your focused intention is to raise private funds, and your fear stops you right in your tracks, then lean into it with these simple steps:

1. Download the *Investment Opportunity One-Sheet* and personalize it with your name and contact information
2. Create a list of 40-90 people from all over the world, whoever comes to mind write their name down… don't prejudge. Keep the list handy and always continue to add to it.
3. Start first with family and friends to build your confidence; you will likely be surprised as to who says 'yes.'
4. Take action; play a game with yourself that you won't go to bed without contacting one new person each day.
5. Create a "First to Know—Private Lender" e-mail list and as you buy and sell new properties send them an update. I even send before and after photos. Some lenders will join you 4-6

months after the initial contact.

6. Follow-up, make sure to follow-up *within a week of the initial contact*. If they say no, ask for a referral. Then add them to your "First to Know" list and periodically continue to follow-up. You are now 'on their radar.'

By taking action you automatically 'lean into your fear.' As a real estate investor, money equals freedom and power. You are free to make tons of offers on great deals, and you have the power to 'make a killing' in the REO market. Once you learn how easy it is to raise private funds, you will discover other money-making opportunities will open for you—like providing lease options. This way, when the economy shifts, you are in control as there are more options you can provide that others can't.

Here is what Matt and Rich said after I challenged them with these six steps...

"We were frustrated with our business and stuck in the crippling mindset that we were inadequate to acquire our own private lenders and expand our business. Eddie challenged us to overcome our reluctance and remove the pretense that we had little to offer our investors. We accepted the time sensitive challenge and got to work quickly. Most of the potential lenders we talked with were not turned off to the idea as we expected. On the contrary, we quickly acquired needed funds and were able to put them to work immediately. Because of Eddie's leadership and encouragement, we have been able to secure over $200,000 of private money without working very hard for it. We are truly grateful."

-Matt and Rich McLean, Knoxville, TN

EFFECTIVE WHOLESALING AND REHABBING

When it comes to selling your REO properties you really have two options; *wholesaling and rehabbing*. As I mentioned above, wholesaling is when you have a property under contract and your goal is to sell it by the time you close the purchase process to another investor—with a profit of $5,000 to $20,000 depending on the property and the deal. The key to wholesaling is to develop an effective list of other investors. This can be done by getting business cards from those at REIA meetings and auctions, constantly networking, as well as placing ads online and in your local papers, or even signs you can place around your neighborhood that read "Handyman Special, Cheap, Cash (with your phone number). All the calls go to our virtual assistant, she adds these names to an e-mail list, and then forwards to them all of your new properties. In addition, you personally call key investors.

The other option is rehabbing, which we've found to be very lucrative. Because we follow the MAO formula, we only purchase properties that produce a profit of $25,000 or more after the purchasing, rehabbing, holding, and investor expenses are deducted. Our spread is typically $30,000 to $45,000.

The key to rehabbing is selecting the right crew, and my background as a construction project manager has definitely proved valuable to create our rehab system. Typically, you're going to need a general contractor (GC), plus electrical, plumbing, air conditioning and heating, painting, kitchen cabinet, roofing, and landscaping contractors. (All need to be licensed except the landscaper.)

If it is your first rehab, I would recommend staying under $25,000 in repairs to get your feet wet. Ask realtors, REIA members, Chamber of Commerce members, etc. about contractors they recommend. Especially in the beginning, I suggest identifying three contractors for each trade and have them bid the project as well as provide references. This way you can compare organic oranges to organic oranges. You will be amazed by the difference in pricing.

Your GC will likely do the majority of the work and needs to be someone you trust. During the inspection period before we buy the house, I always have the GC go to the property with our rehab manger and me to review the inspectors report, confirm the work that needs to be done, and double check the estimate our acquisitionist prepared. [For a copy of our Rehab Estimate & Checklist visit: http://www.NewMastersOfRealEsate.com]

Stephanie Iannotti, a fellow investor and friend, has said *"We produce the nicest rehabs she has ever seen."* Our focused intention when purchasing the next home is how we can make this one the nicest home in the neighborhood... *of course at a rock bottom price!*

Another goldmine in our business is we use the same materials to rehab each project. We typically buy everything from Home Depot and Brands Mart; our cabinet makers use one of two styles we've selected, and we buy our tile from one company. We use the same interior paint, appliances, lighting, ceiling fans, bathroom accessories, etc.; this way we know exactly what our costs are going to be.

When calculating the expenses of the rehab project, keep in mind the square footage of the house. When the house is bigger or in a better location, it will cost more and may require nicer quality finishes. Especially in the beginning, shop around and Google for the best prices. Keep yourself informed on how much a typical bathroom, a kitchen, or square footage of tile costs. Don't stress, as you will learn naturally. To create a little cushion, we always add an extra 20% for miscellaneous expenses. Also, become friends with your contractors and vendors; I found it useful more than once.

Communication is critical with the GC, each contractor, and your rehab manager if you have one. They cannot read your mind and many times have their own opinion as to how the task at hand should be done. This is why walking through the rehab checklist is so important to confirm they are clear on what you want done.

Our goal is to have a rehab project finished within four to six weeks; therefore, we've learned from experience to stay away from properties that have extensive code violations. We refer to code violations such as adding a bathroom without a permit, converting a garage into a bedroom, building an addition that is too close to the property line, city fines for property maintenance, etc. These violations are usually registered with the city/county, so make sure to check them out during the inspection period to know what you are getting into. Usually these repairs can be made easily, but the bureaucracy of the city/county can take months and eat up valuable profits—it's not worth it.

Most contractors require 50% payment to start the job and 50% when completed. Make sure their proposal details the work you've agreed to. In addition, we don't pay the entire balance due until we verify the work has been completed the way instructed. We walk through the project to produce a final punch list to make sure the property is ready to go back on the market.

SELLING YOUR PROPERTY FAST!

Most of our properties go under contract within weeks, if not days, because before we buy, we know what the houses in the neighborhood are selling for and set our ARV at the price that will sell in 30-60 days. So, the day our house goes on the market, it is one of the nicest, lowest priced properties available. We stage our homes with simple pieces of furniture and wall hangings as well as towels and a few accessories in the kitchen and bathrooms.

We list our homes with our realtor on the MLS; however, we place our own "For Sale by Owner" sign in the yard and all of the calls go to our virtual assistant. We've arranged with our realtors a reduced selling commission since we handle all of the calls and hold the open houses. When potential buyers and their realtors call, our virtual assistant gives them the details of the property and lockbox combination.

This way we aren't wasting our time showing the house to people just getting decorating tips; however, we always ask for them to give us a call after they've previewed the house—to make sure it's locked up and we get a sense of their impressions. We are also constantly building our "First to Know—Buyers" list and when we have additional homes in the area, we can call and e-mail those same potential buyers. In addition, we list our homes on our website and various internet sites.

At the property we have a promo sheet of the house, a list of comparable homes that have sold in the area to affirm our price, a sign-in sheet, promo sheet of our other houses on the market, and a loan application if we are providing a lease option or some type of financing on a particular property. When an offer is presented we require a pre-approval letter from the buyer's mortgage company, and once we accept the offer, a letter verifying the escrow deposit has been made is required.

We also change the lockbox combination to ensure we or our rehab manager is at the buyer's inspection and appraisal. This way we can help smooth out any issues that might develop.

Two points to definitely keep in mind:

1. We don't show the buyer's inspector our initial inspection that we order when purchasing the house. Our inspector is really

good and we don't want to give the buyer's inspector any ideas.
2. When meeting the appraiser we always provide the before and after photos with details of the improvements we've made, comparable sales, and the original "As Is" and "After Repair" appraisal that we ordered when purchasing the house. (Make sure *your appraiser* uses comps that will verify the value of the property 60-90 days after his/her initial appraisal has been conducted.) Although technically we are not supposed to give this information to the buyer's appraisers, they usually take it as it makes their job easier.

As I mentioned, curb appeal is critical; therefore we always make sure the house shines on the first impression. Inside, we use great quality materials at the most competitive prices. As a result we typically have our houses under contract in days with a hefty profit to follow.

ATTITUDE IS THE MILLION DOLLAR TICKET

Soon you will find, like we did, that investing in real estate is one of the most rewarding businesses; however… it does present challenges from time to time. I can't tell you how many sleepless nights I've had thinking about all of the possible ways we can transform the next house to make tons of cash. And, we've faced the challenge of being in a new business and having to figure out in the middle of a transaction what the right next step should be. Most of the time we've made the right decision and a few times we haven't. Not knowing what to do next can destroy momentum. That's why in our first year we invested in Ron's "Mastermind Mentoring Program." Today, I'm one of his US and Canadian mentors. There is no reason to do this on your own. Ron's developed a system to teach each step of the way.

Know that as you build your business, what you will find is your attitude is literally a magnet. If you focus on all of the negative, crazy stuff that is happening to you, I guarantee more of the same will soon follow. However, if you learn to live with the "It Is What It Is" factor, you will create a resilience that *only focuses on the possibilities*. You will find amazing solutions to every *challenge* you confront.

Keep your *focused intention* on what it is that you want to accomplish. By doing so, you will be lead to the next right decision. There

are literally millions of dollars that you can make with REOs... You simply have to clarify your focused intention and take action.

SO, LET'S GET STARTED!

From the beginning I've shared that taking action is the critical factor to your success. Literally, you can develop a multi-million dollar a year business just on REOs. However, regardless of the strategy from these chapers on which you decide *to focus your intent*, **taking action is what it is all about.**

I've attempted to provide an overview of the key components that continue to 'make us a killing' in the REO market; however, it is impossible to share it all. That's why I've provided downloads and other helpful resources at: http://www.NewMastersOfRealEstate.com.

In addition, if you would like to learn more of how to incorporate my "focused intention" technique in the physical, mental, emotional, relational, financial, and spiritual aspects of your life, check out my new book - *Living Inside-Out: The Go-To Guide for the Overwhelmed, Overworked & Overcommitted,* where I weave the words of wisdom of sixteen national health and wellness, life-balance, and peak potential experts with what I've learn from my own personal journey. Just go to: http://www.EddieMiller.com.

The REOs are the primary money producer of our business and we've created a great additional income from short sales, subject to's, and options. That's why I suggest identifying what in Ron's programs really work in your areas and give it your primary focus. Then, once you perfect it, you can continue to expand your business.

"Investing in real estate is a Win-Win Sport... we can all make tons of money!"

I say this all the time because I want you to get that regardless of where you are now, you can make tons of money by investing in real estate. Ron, the other mentors, and I, are here to help you make it happen.

So, when one of your fears shows up, know that the same fear has likely shown up for several of the contributing experts in this book, we simply leaned into it and took action.

If you are willing to 'lean in and take action' you can make millions with REOs!

ABOUT EDDIE

Eddie Miller and his partner, Alekxey Sabido, are the owners of Miami Property Solutions LLC—one of the fast growing private real estate investor groups in South Florida.

Eddie and Alekxey are Private Investors, not realtors, and use Private Lenders, not banks, to fund their real estate purchases. They look for "Win-Win-Win" opportunities where the seller, the lender, and the eventual homeowner can all "Win."

They have assembled an impressive team of professionals and together find creative solutions to various real estate challenges. The company specializes in identifying properties that are distressed—in 'short-sale' status or have been foreclosed on and are now owned by the bank.

Miami Property Solutions, LLC is a member of the Dade and Broward Real Estate Investors Associations, the Greater Miami Chamber of Commerce, the Miami Beach Chamber of Commerce and the US–Mexican Chamber of Commerce, as well as has filed Form D under Reg. 506 with the Securities and Exchange Commission.

Eddie is author of the book *Living Inside-Out: The Go-To Guide for the Overwhelmed, Overworked & Overcommitted* and co-author of *The New Masters of Real Estate: Getting Deals Done in the New Economy*, a consultant, a motivational speaker, and host of the popular Answers Are Within teleseminar series.

Alekxey is an acclaimed international visual artist from Mexico and was recently selected as one of the "100 Top Latins in Miami." For the past two seasons his paintings have been featured on the hit show *Keeping Up with the Kardashians* on E!

"Investing in Real Estate is a WIN-WIN SPORT... we can all make tons of money!"

-Eddie Miller

CHAPTER 5
SHORT SALE DEAL: THE LONG TERM BENEFITS OF GOING SHORT WITH A SHORT SALE
LESSON LEARNED

by Robert and Elizabeth Lisk

"The Sky is Falling"…

At least that is what most people think right now in our current market of 2010. House prices are dropping to lows we haven't seen since year 2000, banks are closing up left and right, the banks still in business are not making many loans, and most people would cringe to be an investor in this turbulent time in Real Estate. What I see is opportunity! Great fortunes are to be made in times like these, if you can see through all the perceived chaos - and focus on what the problems are and how you can fix them. A Short Sale is a perfect example of one way to create equity in a property - where under normal circumstances, the numbers would not work for an investor to get involved.

Five years ago most people did not even know what a Short Sale is…

Today, it is a common term in the Real Estate business. For those of you that have not come across this term, a Short Sale is when the lender agrees to accept less than the amount owed to pay off the loan as an alternative to a foreclosure. Simply speaking, the bank is accepting a "Short" amount for the total loan amount due. In the current market, with house prices continuing to plummet, a Short Sale can be a great option for someone facing foreclosure. It will give them the opportunity to walk away from their house and debt if the lender will accept a Short Sale offer. As an investor we can create equity in a deal. As a homeowner, you have a chance at having tens of thousands or hundreds of thousands of dollars potentially wiped off from your loan, keeping you out of foreclosure - which will harm your credit.

In my business, I believe I am helping to stabilize the market by preventing a foreclosure and reselling the home to someone at a great price that is still below current market value.

One of my past Short Sale homeowners called me the week before Christmas in a panic about her current situation… She was a single mother with two children and one on the way, recently divorced, and left with the house and a mortgage she could not pay on her current salary. I met her on a very snowy day in Chicago where it redeemed it's nickname, "The Windy City." It definitely was a day that if you didn't really need to go out of your house … you wouldn't.

Nonetheless, we got together and we signed the agreements for a Short Sale, as she was very motivated to get her problems resolved. I assured her that I would do my best to stop the foreclosure on her home, however I did not make any promises. In the next two months my Short Sale Packet was received by the mitigator at the bank and I requested the BPO to be ordered - which is an interior appraisal completed by a Real Estate Agent of the bank's choice. Within a few weeks it was ordered, and I met the agent at the house to give her a packet showing (1) my offer to the bank, (2) the homeowner's hardship letter, and (3) the current 'comps' of the homes in the surrounding area. This is the most important part of the entire short sale process, because the bank will base their entire decision of whether or not a discount will be given, and how much of a discount will be given to the property, almost solely upon the BPO. If the BPO comes in too high… then you will probably not be able to make enough of a spread to have the numbers work for you. If you are able to get it in low enough, you will be able to create a spread between what the bank will take and what an end buyer will pay when you flip the property to them. the BPO agent looked at my package and understood that someone was going to go into foreclosure if I was not able to make this offer work with the bank. The point of this is getting them to help with the numbers to support your offer to the bank. It is important to understand that we, as investors, are not asking them to do anything illegal, but rather to work within their guidelines to get the number as low as possible - so that I can help this single mother from an unfortunate situation that she is in... she is losing her house and facing a foreclosure, which is not good either for her or the bank.

The BPO was completed and within two weeks I was speaking with the mitigator about my cash offer and working towards getting an acceptance letter to move to closing. In the meantime, the house was listed with one of my realtors to secure an end buyer. Within a few short weeks, an end buyer was in place with closing on the horizon. In touching base with the homeowner on how the process was going, she *casually* mentioned to me about a personal loan from a friend of $6,600 that might be attached to the house. I wondered why my preliminary title search didn't show it, but it didn't. Knowing that title has to be cleared so that the closing can take place, I ordered a full title search on the property. In doing so, the personal loan did show up on title of the house. These can be simple to remove and get a discount.. ... or sometimes not so much, depending on the disposition of the person with whom they have the promissory note. There can be personal grudge and they do not want to discount but rather want the full amount or cause the homeowner to face foreclosure.

Having me pay the full promissory amount would put me out of my buying criteria and would kill the deal. I started looking for this person through the attorney that created the note... no luck. After three weeks of going back and forth with the attorney, I asked the homeowner if they knew where he was. She knew a friend of a friend that might know where he was. So I contacted him, and remarkably, within an hour he called me back. Amazing when you share with someone that you have money to give them how quickly they will call you back. We negotiated back and forth over another two weeks to arrive at a payoff of $3,000.00 for him to release his note with the homeowner. He was marginally happy with the amount, and so was I, but we were both able to agree and that allowed me to move forward to closing.

For those of you new to the business, here is a huge lesson to learn when it comes to personal promissory notes. Of course this gentleman wanted to meet me later that day to receive his money for the pay off. Under NO circumstances do you give him money BEFORE you close. You meet with them to get a Release signed stating your agreement that you will pay him $3000.00 AT CLOSING for his release of the note, and have it satisfy his debt with the homeowner. If you pay them ahead of time, you run the risk of being out that money if by chance you don't close on the property. We met the next day and signed the agreement. At this point, I am only days away from getting my approval from the bank, and finalizing last minute details before closing.

Next, make sure when your homeowner is vacating the house, that a few things happen:

1. They leave the house in 'move-in' condition. *
2. No appliances are to be taken out of the property. They need to be reminded of this right before they are moving out. * Ask me how I know this!
3. Garbage and items they do not want are to be removed by them, not left in the house. *Ask me how I know this!!

   *All of these points should be a part of your Short Sale paperwork that they agree to and sign in the beginning with you. If you do this, you will save thousands of dollars - preventing you from having to hire someone to remove garbage and furniture and anything else they leave in the house! If they decide to take an appliance or two, again you will be responsible for getting something back in place, because at this point you have a end buyer and have signed an agreement with them – stating that those items are in fact part of your purchase and sale agreement with them.

So now my homeowner has found a place to stay and I am ready to close. The day arrives and I have not seen the homeowner for months. She greets me with a hug letting me know how happy she is to move on from the house and the debt. I negotiated $128,111.00 off of her and her ex-husband's name with a Full Satisfaction. Do Short Sales Work? Absolutely... Did I do a good thing for a couple that hit upon hard times? Yes.

We signed all the documents at my attorney's office and within an hour I was re-selling it to a first time homebuyer who was thrilled to get her first home at a great price.

I'd say we all came out winners. I stopped foreclosure on one couple, and got the bank to write the debt off, then resold it to another person for a great deal.... And oh yes.., the best part... I made some money in the middle. It was a good day...

Robert and Elizabeth Lisk
Home Solutions Investments LLC

ABOUT ROBERT AND ELIZABETH

Robert and Elizabeth Lisk of Home Solutions have been buying and selling houses since the early 80's.. Their expertise has been with short sales, rehabbing to flip, buying bank owned properties, and building custom residential homes.

Robert has bought, sold, rehabbed, remodeled and built custom homes for hundreds of customers.. We solve people's problems, and in the process buy their house. We take what is causing them to worry and find a solution, creating pleasure over their pain. Robert received his Civil Engineering degree from USC, and his MBA from Lake Forest Graduate School of Management.

Elizabeth has been in real estate since early 1990's. She loves being able to help customers of hers out of a difficult situation. She also loves taking an ugly house and turning into something spectacular. Elizabeth received her Bachelor's degree from Western Illinois University.

Robert and Elizabeth live in Lake Forest, IL, and have two exceptionally happy and beautiful daughters.

www.chicagolandwebuyhouses.com
www.shortsaleforeclosureil.com
www.myshortsalesmadeeasy.com
www.homesolutions-buy.com
www.homesolutions-sell.com

Home Solutions
825 S Waukegan Rd. A8 Suite 152
Lake Forest, IL 60045
Office: 847-510-6676

CHAPTER 6
EXUBERANT INNOCENCE TO ETHICAL MATURITY - MORAL TRANSITIONS IN INVESTING

by Dr. Grant Kilpatrick

I. BASIC REAL ESTATE INVESTMENT CONCEPTS

What motivates the 'normal' person to invest in real estate? I use the word 'normal' since in my 50 years of investing (I like to think that I started my training playing Monopoly at about 10 years of age!) I have seen very few people that have invested successfully in real estate relative to the rest of the population. So the successful investor is 'out of the ordinary' or is not in the range of 'normal experience' for a person seeking out a career in real estate investing.

Success in real estate requires a certain skill set, some of which are inherent in a person's personality. These would be self-motivation, analytical skills, ability to control the fear of potentially massive financial loss, ability to take decisive action, a contrarian attitude of investing relative to the population, and a desire to act outside of one's normal comfort zone.

Then there is the learned skill set required of managers—the ability to collect information and sort it into relevant and irrelevant, simple mathematical skills, and people management skills.

Matching these inherent and acquired skills with a generous dose of what I call a healthy FQ (Financial Quotient), we have the makings of a person who can 'weather any storms' the market can churn up.

But what is it that pushes such people to 'step off the cliff', to see if they can fly or 'chance being dashed to financial ruin on the rocks below', if they fall?

II. THE PUSH

The push into real estate investing can be as varied as each person's situation demands. For me, it was the fact that I needed a 'pension plan.' Although I made a good living in my professional career, I found it difficult to set money aside for my long-term future needs. Plus, the thrill of the "game" to be played beckoned me. I was ultra-successful at monopoly as a child and adolescent—no one could beat me if I kept the game going long enough. But as an adult, the game that invited me was one of real buildings, real money, real debt and the potential of real loss. This risk factor and the adrenalin surge that comes with it - caused me to thrive.

For others the push can be the loss of financial stability through divorce, loss of a job (...Just Over Broke!), or low points in the market cycles. These low points (early 70's, early 80's, early 90's, 2008-09) cause uncertainty and wreak havoc with people's financial plans. I had lunch with a friend recently that had to suspend his retirement plans because of the 40 per cent drop in the market. He then withdrew his remaining capital from the market, missing the 2009-10 market gain, however slow. He was seeking a solution and was wondering about the potential of real estate as an investment vehicle to regain his financial stability.

III. THE OPPORTUNITY

As a young professional, I was succeeding quickly and had set aside a small down payment for a house. I had already purchased my own office building after stumbling across a vacant building with a motivated seller.

(*Principle #1: Own, don't rent*).

I had already formed a vague notion of purchasing an apartment building so that at sometime in the future the renters would have paid the mortgage and I would live on the income generated from it. In fact, I mentioned that idea to my father when we parked next to an apartment building one Sunday.

(*Principle #2: Speak out your goals aloud to someone else, thereby committing your subconscious to the goal.*)

It was a year later that I drove by that same apartment building, which now was sporting a "Power of Sale" sign. The mortgage holder was foreclosing. I called and asked how many units were in the building. The answer intimidated me—"Twelve." Remember, I did not have a house yet, and the only money I had was a small down payment. However, I gathered the information, analyzed my capabilities and the strengths and weaknesses of both the building and myself. (What's the worst that can happen? How would I deal with it?)

The fact that the mortgage holder intended to force the sale that week caused an additional 'push.' I saw the sign Tuesday, analyzed data Wednesday, viewed the building Thursday, and hired a lawyer friend of mine to come to my home on Friday night after work to write up an offer. (The Offer: My $5000 down payment, and seller financing for the balance.) The offer was submitted Saturday at 9:00 a.m. By 10:00 a.m. I was the new owner of a 12-unit downtown apartment building.

So, I purchased my first investment property with virtually no knowledge and no courses on investing or seller financing. I just collected and analyzed the information. But because of the time frame set by the seller, I was forced to **take action**.

I call this period in an investor's life "exuberant innocence." I was very excited and too innocent about what **could** happen. The decisive step was taking action. The result was that I acquired a several hundred thousand dollar property for $5000 and about five hours of my time. I accepted the risk and learned the rest.

(*Principle #3: If one dwells on all the things that can go wrong, the opportunity will go away.*)

During the next year, I purchased four acres of lakefront lot property, then found another waterfront property a lot closer to my office with a home already on it. My exuberant innocence was at work.

IV. COINCIDENCE OR DIVINE INTERVENTION?

My professional practice was growing, and I really enjoyed helping people. But I was paying mortgages on three properties. I was musing about concentrating on my practice and getting out of real estate investment while on a plane to Chicago for a professional seminar. I had just about decided on that path when a real estate investor presented during the seminar. I think he was invited to speak for an hour midway through the conference to break up the intensity of the conference and because he was very entertaining. His topic? "Buying Properties With No Money Down."

As a result of his presentation, I saw greater opportunity with no real downside. I purchased his book and tapes and reset my path—I would learn more, and do real estate as a hobby!

Within a short time I had found and purchased a multi-residential/commercial property. But in working up the offer, with my newfound knowledge of how to do a no-money-down deal, I was working on a further angle. If no-money-down offers were possible, how about deals that generated cash on closing? One evening with this thought in mind, in a few minutes I worked out the wording of a new offer which would end up generating about 10% of the purchase price in cash in my pocket on closing. Again, finding a motivated seller was the key. I consulted with my lawyer and accountant asking if there was anything illegal or immoral in this. They said no, as long as I wasn't going to walk away from the mortgage. So I closed that deal and flew to Hawaii for a vacation.

(*Principle #4: Reward yourself for success*).

However, I really wondered if this cash-generating close was a fluke of nature or of the business or not. So I found another multi-residential building and formulated another offer to generate 15% of the purchase price in cash in my pocket on closing. That was a successful buy. My conclusion: No fluke. I can make cash flow by purchasing real estate!

At that point, my family was growing, cash flow was great, and I doubled my professional practice through the severe recession of the early 80's. Life was good. I decided to take my young family on a 15-month world trip. I was all set to go. One month before I left, I received a telephone call 'out of the blue' asking me to purchase another 16-unit building. I almost declined, but, realizing the seller was really motivated, I decided to proceed. This time I had no ready cash, the seller needed 10 % down for his taxes, and since there was no time before I left the country to secure institutional financing, I needed other sources of capital. I quickly found three other investors to put up the down payment and the seller financed the 90 per cent balance.

I left the country in September and the deal closed in November while I was on an island somewhere in the South Pacific. When I returned to Canada over a year later, one investor wanted her money out, so I purchased her share which gave me 50% ownership. By the way, that building has not required any more of the investors' money to run it since the day we purchased it.

(*Principle #5: When opportunity knocks, find the way to open the door!*)

V. THE NEXT STEP—CHARACTER DEVELOPMENT

As you might imagine, at this point as a young professional with my net worth growing rapidly, I was quite pleased with myself. Life was good. One day while reading about "craftiness" not being a good character trait, I agreed that I did not desire this trait for myself. I paused reading to meditate on that for a few moments pondering to myself whether I had ever been "crafty." Immediately, the real estate deals described above where I had closed the deals and put substantial cash in my pocket on closing with no output of my own cash came to mind.

I had not disclosed the intricacies of those deals to the sellers. I realized that by not disclosing this, a deal was placed in the realm of 'craftiness.' I did not want this crafty practice as a legacy on my character. Therefore, I decided that I would not use this strategy in the future without full disclosure to the seller.

(*Principle #6: Always make full disclosure to the seller.*)

Hence, only as time proceeded, and after some introspection on the effects of my behavior on myself and on the community around me, did

I come to a measure of what I call "ethical maturity."

Over the years, my experience with real estate investment has brought me much success, but it also brought me this lesson: As a real estate investor I must be careful to be fair, ethical and open with buyers and sellers if I want to live in harmony and peace with the community in which I live. To do otherwise is to risk my own peace, joy and contentment—which, in the game of real estate investment, is the ultimate reward.

ABOUT GRANT

Dr. Grant A. Kilpatrick

- Raised as a farm boy in South Western Ontario, Canada. Graduated with a B.Sc. (Chemistry Major) from University of Western Ontario - where a business course was a high point of his studies.

- Went on to get his doctor of chiropractic in Toronto.

- Married to Joanne his wife of 33 years and has three grown children- two daughters and one son. One daughter is a teacher and ESL specialist, and one is communications and media director with the foremost environmental NGO, Canada. His son is in commercial aviation management studies while managing a student housing business.

- Grant has purchased and managed several multi-residential and/or commercial properties since 1978 while running a busy health practice.

- He has also taken time to travel the world on an 18 month sabbatical with his family. He has studied at a masters-level counselling program in Switzerland and Hawaii and all this was done while operating his real estate business through the strength of delegation.

- After retiring from his health practice in 2008, because of structural complications two years after a compression back fracture in 2006, he has obtained further real estate knowledge from his mentor Ron LeGrand while renovating his home property on one of the most beautiful waterways in the world in the District of Muskoka in Central Ontario, Canada where celebrities, wealthy industrialists and entrepreneurs go to play, rest and relax.

- He is a charter member of the Federation of Rental Housing Providers Ontario (FRPO) and keeps informed of legal changes and information pertinent to the businesses from several publications.

CHAPTER 7
THE MOST EFFECTIVE SOCIAL MEDIA SALES TOOL OF ALL*

(*and one of the oldest! How the 24-hour pre-recorded message can build trust, sell real estate, and make your life a whole lot easier!)

by Jay Conner

Every marketer is selling the virtues of social media. Twitter, Facebook…they're big online resources that are being used 'to the max' by everyone with a business. Real estate, of course, is no exception.

But I want to talk about using what I consider a form of social media that predates Facebook. It even predates MySpace. As a matter of fact, it even predates personal computers and websites.

It's the 24-hour pre-recorded phone message.

"Hold on, Jay," you're saying. "How is that social media? Where's the 'social' part of this? You can't tweet, you can't post on a wall, nor can you update your status with a pre-recorded message. You can't even look up that weird guy I went to Junior High School with to see if he's out of prison yet."

71

Well, first of all, I really don't even want to deal with that weird guy in prison. Second of all, the pre-recorded 24-hour message *is* social media to me. It's been one of the most effective, automatic sales tools I've ever used. As a matter of fact, I credit a lot of my success in real estate in North Carolina to it.

But how is it social media?

Think about how people use Facebook. You can find out about people before you decide you're going to accept them as a "friend." And you're not going to take that step unless you have some degree of trust in who the person is.

That's exactly how I've used the pre-recorded message over the years. People can listen to the information I or one of my associates provide in a totally non-threatening way. They can hang up at any time. They have control over the situation. So they're more comfortable *seeking out* the information.

In other words, even though the conversation is decidedly one-sided, it's still the beginning of a relationship. I give them the freedom to choose if they want to talk to a live person about the property in question or not. That freedom in turn empowers more potential buyers to make the call, knowing no one's going to personally hard sell them. It ends up as a win-win for both my real estate company and the customer.

It didn't start out that way. No, I first began to use the pre-recorded message as a necessity.

LISTEN FOR THE TONE...

When I began my career as a real estate investor, I had a huge problem. I was only doing it part-time. I still had a "real" job.

So, when I put my classified real estate ads in the newspaper, with my cell phone number listed for contact information, I wasn't able to answer most of the calls. I just wasn't available because of my job, and I couldn't afford, at that point, to abandon my steady 9-5 income. And many people simply wouldn't leave a message. I was losing a lot of leads – and probably a lot of business.

Then in 2004, I happened across master marketer Dan Kennedy's "No

B.S. – Business Success" book - in it was the idea of using a 24-hour pre-recorded message. Meaning that, at any time, day or night, a potential buyer or seller could find out more detailed information about the property as well as financing options, in a tightly scripted message, without me having to worry about missing the call.

And also, to be honest, without me having to say the same thing over and over to whoever called.

Sometimes, 'necessity is the mother not only of invention, but of success.' What I immediately discovered, to my surprise, was that once I replaced my cell phone number in the ad with the words, "Call our free 24 hour recorded message," I suddenly was getting *three times the response* of my previous classified ads!

That's what you call a nice surprise!

After some thought and some research, I found there were two reasons for the sudden increased ROI of my classifieds.

The #1 reason was that it's actually been proven that a publicly accessed phone message is more credible than talking to a live salesperson. People must figure a salesperson will say anything to get business, while a recorded message is "on the record" and has to stick to the facts.

The #2 reason is what I talked about earlier – the caller feels like they're under no obligation; they can bail out of the message at any time and don't have to worry about a live hard sell. They are able to find out the facts without dealing with a salesperson.

To me, the 24 hour recorded message is the best kept marketing secret of the last 20 years. There are very few real estate and other business entrepreneurs using it anymore – as I said, everyone's moved on to Facebook, Twitter, texting and other newer methods. If you look in the real estate classifieds in my area, you'll quickly see that I'm the only person using the words "24 hour recorded message" in their ads. Which is fine by me!

There are 10 very good reasons I'm going to continue to use this old school "social media" to build my real estate business. With apologies to David Letterman…

THE TOP TEN REASONS THE PRE-RECORDED MESSAGE WORKS FOR ME:

1. As I noted, I get three times the response by using the message as my response device in my classifieds. It also allows me to be four times as productive, since, again, my staff and I don't have to keep giving out the same information over and over to different people.
2. The ROI is amazing. It's VERY low cost to use.
3. It's easy to use. My marketing is basically on autopilot.
4. It's very effective in measuring the results of my advertising. All of my marketing is measured and tracked, so I know what's worth spending money on and what's not.
5. It saves me and my staff a tremendous amount of time and money. Just by generating a short two-to-three line classified ad, and then recording a more detailed phone message about specific properties, I can educate and give out a lot of information without having to print it in the paper or in a direct mail piece.
6. This is a good one. With the hotline system I use, I can capture the phone numbers of the people calling the pre-recorded message - *whether they leave a number or not!* That holds true even if they're using Caller ID block. It's legal because, by deciding they wanted to call me, I now have the right to talk to them about my business. This means that *every response equals a true lead.*
7. By using different extensions on the main phone number for different recorded messages, I can tell which particular ad is generating the most response. Again, this helps tremendously with marketing decisions down the road.
8. I'm only capturing quality leads – people who are interested in making a real estate deal. They're good to market to with follow-up calls.
9. Callers can access a real live person at any time during the pre-recorded message. That means, if they like what they hear, they merely push the button they're instructed to and they'll be switched to a live salesperson who will be able to give more information and even schedule an appointment to see the property in question.
10. No busy signals – we never, ever have to worry about missing a call. Again – NO LEAD IS LOST! And, obviously, it doesn't

matter if your actual office is open or closed. Your system is working around the clock for you. And it's a good thing, as we get as many calls after 10 pm as we do at any other time.

MAKING THE MESSAGE WORK FOR YOU

The best way to begin using the pre-recorded message is with a very short teaser-type classified ad that will spark a prospect to call.

Here's an example of an ad I'd use to interest people who want to sell their property:

I buy houses. Cash offer in 90 minutes guaranteed. Any condition. You choose the closing date! Call 24 hour free recorded message – 1 xxx-xxx-xxxx

Here's another example of an ad used to generate buyers' interest:

Owner-financing! Or lease/option. Or rent-to-own. No banks needed! 4 nice homes to choose from. Morehead City, Beaufort and Newport areas. 24 hour free recorded list and directions. 1-xxx-xxxx-xxxx

In that last ad, you'll notice I talked about a recorded list and directions, rather than just a recorded message. That's to play on people's curiosity factor – they'll want to know where are these houses? I know that this works, because when I've used the word "directions" in an ad, the response rate went up. It's the kind of information usually withheld to get the person to talk to the real estate agent "live."

Once you've begun to use the pre-recorded message, there are a lot more tricks and great techniques on how to maximize its advantages to capture and convert leads that I've learned over the years – and I'm happy to share in this chapter.

10 INSIDERS' SECRETS
FOR USING THIS MAGICAL TOOL

1. "The more you tell – the more you sell."

There's a myth that shorter messages work better – that's simply NOT TRUE. Most of my scripts for the pre-recorded messages are about a minute long. And I always put the messages through my TMI process

– I <u>T</u>est them, <u>M</u>easure their response and <u>I</u>mprove them. I check how many people hang up half way through, how many people opt to talk to a live person during the call, and how many willingly leave their contact info. *The biggest sin here is to be boring* – but providing useful information <u>builds trust and creates more interest</u>.

2. Do *not* ask for the caller's phone number in your message.

Ask for just their name, address and email. It's been proven that, when you don't ask for their phone number, they feel like they have more control and are more willing to leave their other contact info. And besides, you're capturing their phone number anyway!

3. Allow immediate access to a live representative.

I give callers the option and the instructions on how to talk with me or my reps at any time during the message, and I will give that option several times during the call. If they're that anxious to find out more about what you have to offer, you should 'strike while the iron is hot.'

4. Put the pre-recorded message number on the back of your business card.

If they want to find out more about what you have to offer, again, its a non-threatening way to do it - and you'll increase the number of responses you'll get from your card.

5. Immediately call back all callers whether they leave a message or not.

I have two virtual assistants - one to talk to sellers, one to talk to potential buyers. If the prospect who called for the recorded message doesn't choose to talk to someone or leave their info, the appropriate assistant gets an instant text or email message to call the person's phone number. This actually impresses most callers – they see us as being on top of their business. And the other thing we do during the callback is be very softsell, low pressure and *nice*. They might say something like, "Hi, this is Glenda with Jay Conner and I was just notified that you called about so-and-so. I just wanted to let you know that I'm here to answer any questions you might have." This helps build trust and the relationship.

6. Measure the ROI of each ad.

Would you buy stock in a company and never check the stock price again to see how it's doing? Well, what's the point in paying for marketing if you don't know how well it's working? That's why I put different extension numbers on each classified ad - to measure their effectiveness. That way I can run a report on exactly what my cost per response per ad is, and my cost per sale on marketing. This is important, because you can never be sure what works. I recently ran a test on an ad about a home I had for sale – I listed a great many benefits and it cost me more than most of my other ads. But I was completely wrong, because it brought in the least amount of results! Knowing that will save me a lot of money down the line.

7. Use your generated leads from the message system to build a buyers' list.

Use the contact information you gather from your recorded messages for follow-up marketing – it's a waste to gather quality leads without building a marketing database from them.

8. Put these exact words in your ad – "24 hour free recorded message."

Each one of those words is important – I know, because I've tested them thoroughly. If you don't tell them plainly and clearly it works around the clock and it's recorded, they don't know. Those are the words that create a high response. Use them!

9. Don't let the sound of your own voice stop you!

You might not like your own speaking voice, so you may avoid using this system. Don't! All services offer the option of having someone else with a more professional voice record your outgoing message for you, so feel free to use it. Keep in mind, however, you may connect more by using your own non-professional voice, as you'll be more "real" to them. Have objective honest people evaluate how you really sound, not how you think you sound.

10. Use a local number instead of a national toll-free number if possible.

Some services now offer the choice of using a number with a local area code, rather than an 800 or 877 national number. If yours does, go for the local one. Again, it feels more personal and less threatening to prospective callers. Oh, and speaking of services, I use two great ones - Automated Marketing Solutions (check them out at AutomatedMarketingSolutions.com) and PATLive (at PATLive.com).

You still might feel that using a pre-recorded message as a lynchpin for your marketing is just too old-fashioned and won't work in today's online-dominated world. Well, I recently hired a Craigslist specialist to insert an ad into that popular internet classifieds website that offered an option for contacting me – email or my 24 hour recorded message. Well, 27% still went with the 24 hour message for the first contact.

And that's why I always make sure to put that message phone number in all of my media – print ads, websites, online web promotions, yellow page ads, postcards...*everything*. It's still the first choice for many responding people.

Direct mail is no exception. I currently have an eight letter sequence I send out to people in pre-foreclosure. After the first two letters, which are designed to look like some one just drove by the house and wanted to buy it, I introduce the 24 hour recorded message with the third letter.

Now, by the time I do the fifth letter, I've given them many other ways to contact me as well – but the 24 hour number is always one of them. That's because I always make sure to put that 24 hour recorded message into the mix of whatever marketing I'm doing. I'll be honest – it's not the entire answer to any marketing program. But in my world, it almost always is.

And I'll prove it – if you're interested in seeing some of my pre-recorded scripts or finding out more about my proprietary foreclosure mailing system I just mentioned...well, then you should just call my 24 hour recorded message at 1-877-288-8753, ext.2665

You see – I practice what I preach!

ABOUT JAY

Jay Conner is a proven real estate investment leader. He locates, buys, and sells multiple real estate deals, even in the new economy. Jay is a recognized investment genius, having graduated as a Master in Real Estate Investing; and he accepted Ron LeGrand's invitation into the prestigious Platinum Inner Circle.

Without using his own money or credit, Jay maximizes creative methods to move properties for substantial profits with little to no risk. "Jay is a real estate magician," noted a business networking associate. "He works seemingly magical deals for buyers and sellers alike."

Beyond his own success, Jay's passion in real estate is to enlighten and inspire other investors. To that end, Jay mentors fellow investors across the United States and Canada. His consulting goes far beyond elementary "how to" techniques. Jay teaches an entrepreneur to transform a Real Estate Investing Business into an "Automatic Transaction Machine," thus allowing his students to achieve their life goals: Financial Independence and the Freedom to enjoy what's really important to them.

Hand-in-hand with his one-on-one mentoring, Jay shares his insights at seminars as a leading expert on private lending, marketing, business development and ethical business practices.

Jay pours his talents and energies into numerous activities. He is President of Conner Properties and EZ Mortgages, plus a former CEO of Leader Homes. He is also co-developing The Coves at Newport, a community of condominiums along the Atlantic Coast. In 1997 Jay formed Encore Music, a private record label, where he records original piano compositions and produces other artists. He also founded and directs The Carolina Chords, an *a capella* chorus in great demand. Jay and his wife, Carol, currently reside in Newport, NC.

Ready to jump start your real estate investing career? Contact Jay Conner, Real Estate Master and Mentor, at 252.725.3360 or

connermentor@yahoo.com.

CHAPTER 8
NO MONEY REAL ESTATE INVESTING

by Jim Zaspel

Hang on a second here! Isn't that an oxymoron? By the definition of the word, doesn't someone have to have money to "invest" in something? Ok, you do have to have a little money. You must have ten dollars for the deposit.

The concept I just described to you has made hundreds of thousands and even millions of dollars for many people. Contrary to popular opinion, no matter what kind of residential real estate deal you do, you should get paid for what you know, not for how much you spend or the amount of debt you guarantee from a bank.

Now if you are going to earn an income based on what you know about real estate, then doesn't it make sense to learn as much as possible? This is where many people fail. People fail to invest in *themselves*, so they fall into the trap that has gotten thousands of investors into financial ruin – namely leveraging their wallets and personal credit instead of their brains and continuing to work hard instead of smart.

What I want to do here is give a brief overview of the four basic ways to invest in real estate without using your own money or personally guaranteeing any debt. Then I am going to focus on how to actually find the motivated sellers and buyers with none of your own money, on marketing. Does that sound good to you? Well then, let's get started.

HERE ARE THE FOUR BASIC WAYS TO BUY AND SELL REAL ESTATE THE "NO-MONEY" WAY:

1. Wholesale

To wholesale a property you get a property "under contract" at a discounted price - with just a ten or perhaps a hundred dollar deposit. Usually the reason a house is discounted so steeply is because the property is in dire need of repair, but sometimes the property is in fine condition and the seller is just really motivated to sell the house quickly and is willing to sell it at a discounted price in order to do so. Once you have it under contract, find someone who is willing to pay more for the property than your contracted price. At closing, you will get paid an Assignment Fee for assigning your contract to buy that piece of real estate to your buyer. In this scenario, your buyer buys it directly from your seller so that you never have to bring the funds to closing — you simply make the 'middle man' cut. The key to successfully wholesaling a property is to get it under contract at a big enough discount so that there is plenty of profit left in the deal for the person buying from you. I'll never forget cashing the check from my first wholesale deal, I made $13,800 on my first wholesale deal!

2. Option

This is more or less the same as Wholesaling, except that a different agreement is used, and it is generally used on 'pretty' (no repairs needed) houses. When optioning a property, you most often will be finding an owner-occupant buyer — that is, someone who wants to purchase the property to live in it.

3. Subject To

This has made me the most money of any of the strategies. This technique is generally used when buying a 'pretty' house and selling it to an owner occupant. Buying a property "subject to" the underlying loan is to have the existing loan stay in the name of the seller, but the deed transfers to the buyer's name. You can then sell this property on a Lease-Purchase or Owner-Financing program. What's so powerful about this method is that it not only enables you to buy houses without cash or credit, but it also enables you to sell properties at lightening speed because your buyers don't need to qualify for a loan from a bank.

4. Rehab

Here you purchase run-down property with private money. Private money is money that is borrowed from a private individual. When borrowing private money to buy a 'fixer-upper', be sure to borrow enough to cover the purchase price, repair costs, and a small slush fund.

That is all the detail I am going to go into regarding the actual transactions. For the rest of this chapter, I am going to assume that you know the fundamentals of these four basic methods of buying and selling real estate.

For any investor, especially someone just starting out, the biggest costs of doing business are marketing costs — marketing to find motivated sellers and motivated buyers. There are many great marketing methods promoted that have a significant cost to them, and I have used many of them. They are effective, but like I said, they cost money.

Here is what you need to do *right now*: get rid of any notion that you have to pay out of pocket for your marketing. It's simply not necessary. Of course in some instances I pay for my deals, but it is in the form of a referral or finder's fee, and any such fee is paid only if/when I have been paid on that specific deal. The point of all this is to reduce your monthly outgo, yet have a constant flow of sellers and buyers coming to you, wanting to do business.

Next, I am going to list several ways to find or locate motivated sellers and several more ways to do the same with finding motivated buyers of real estate - all of which will require none or very little of your own money. But this I assure you, that every one of them if done properly will produce phenomenal results! Some of these methods are over-lapping, but first let's talk about getting sellers to come to you.

1. Marketing Partners

These are simply other investors that *are* spending money to get leads (prospects) contacting them via a website, phone, or email. If you do what I talked about at the beginning of this chapter and educate yourself in real estate investing so that you know how to handle any deal that comes at you, then you will put yourself above the crowd, and once people at your local REIA meetings discover all the different types of transactions you are doing, you won't be able to handle all the many leads that come to you.

2. REIA (Real Estate Investor Association) Meetings

You must attend every single investors meeting that you possibly can! Not only is this going to be your best source of marketing partners, but you will find qualified buyers, people that want to lend private money, and people that currently own properties that they want you to buy.

3. Referrals

There is an unlimited number of ways to get people referring business to you, but I am going to share with you what my mentor, Jon, told me when I was starting out. He said, "Jim, you've got to let people know what you do. Put the lettering on your vehicle, wear the clothes with your company name on them, go to every REIA meeting you can, make sure all your friends and family know that you buy and sell houses." Then he said, "What you want to do is make such a name for yourself so that when anyone who has come in contact with you wants to buy or sell a house, *you* are the first person they think of." These simple yet fundamental words have had a larger impact on my business than anything else Jon EVER told me, and as a result of following his advice, people are constantly referring their friends and family members to me. Of course I only just listed a few out of *many* ways to accomplish this, but like Jon said, you must "brand" yourself.

4. Online

This is the most simple, yet one of the most powerful methods of finding deals for free. When you look up FSBO (For Sale By Owner) ads online, be sure to look for key words in the ad headings. Words or phrases to keep an eye out for are *foreclosure, must sell now, motivated seller, burnt-out landlord wants to retire, estate, relocation, divorce, jobloss, immediate occupancy available, owner will finance,* and *lease-purchase.* There are many good websites out there on which to find FSBO's, but ones such as Craigslist.com, kijiji.com, postlets.

com, fsbo.com, forsalebyowner.com, and ownerwillcarry.com are some of the most productive websites to call ads from if you are going to call FSBO's.

5. Newspapers and Other Offline Periodicals

I know what you're thinking, you're thinking that newspapers cost money. If you want to get it early in the morning, I'm sure it does, but people leave newspapers sitting around all the time. If you want to get a hold of used newspapers, just take a stroll through any public transportation station, restaurant, or coffee shop and I'm sure you'll find plenty of them. You can also work something out with a convenience store manager to get some of their old newspapers. I know – this sounds weird. But if you are determined to make money in real estate without using your own money, then you must be willing to think outside the box.

6. Realtors

When you work with properties listed in the MLS, most of the time you are going to be dealing with properties that need repairs and that require cash. If you line up your private money lender and can put up a $1,000 deposit on a house (don't worry, you'll get it back at closing), then the MLS is a great source for finding deals. The trick is that you must be able to close on the deals that you sign contracts on.

Let's recap. First we established that it does *not* take money to make money in real estate. Then we learned a few basic methods of buying and selling houses, and finally we learned how to find the deals that are worth doing by finding motivated sellers. Whatever you do, do not forget the second point, namely, that you must first *learn* how to do creative real estate transactions before you can do them. Of course you don't need to know much in order to wholesale a property, but if you want to do all the various types of deals that I have mentioned, you should invest (yes, with your own money) in real estate education.

SO, WHAT ARE WE MISSING? WHAT COMPONENT OF THE BUSINESS HAVE I LEFT OUT?

We still need to discuss how to sell all these houses that you are getting! You will notice that some of the best methods of finding buyers for your properties that cost little or no money are going to overlap with the methods I have shown you for finding sellers. This is the great part of networking — you never know what each new relationship you create will turn into. The possibilities are endless!

1. Online

Use all of the websites I gave you for finding sellers to list your properties. The best ones are free. I have also successfully used Ebay to sell houses, but it does have its own challenges, so make sure that you know their rules and regulations before you spend money listing a property for sale on their website.

2. Loan Officers

When you buy a property subject to the underlying loan by simply taking over the seller's debt, typically the best way to sell that house is on a lease-option or with owner financing. In either case, your target market is the part of society that can afford a home, but that does not have good enough credit to go get a traditional loan for the house. In a down market, the vast majority of applications that loan officers get are denied for a loan. That's where investors like me come in. I simply tell the loan officer that if he puts me in touch with his rejected applicants that have a significant (five percent or greater) deposit, I will sell houses to those individuals on lease-purchase programs. In such a scenario, the tenant-buyer would put up a significant deposit and begin making lease payments to me. During the lease period I will work with an agency to restore their credit, so that within six to eighteen months, that tenant-buyer will have the credit to get the loan that they originally applied for and were rejected. Of course I then will direct that person to get the loan for the home from the loan officer that originally referred them to me. The point here is that I show the loan officer how to turn the leads or prospects that he is currently throwing away into a real and significant source of income at no added cost to him! It's a win-win for everyone.

3. Social Media

If you have a large following on networks such as Facebook, Twitter, Myspace, and YouTube, and you know how to properly use those networks, there are very few things that you can do that will increase your brand image more than this as *the* go-to person for all real estate solutions. The point of it is to let people know what you do and make them want to hear everything you have to say, *without* being a constant salesperson. A great thing to do is to post videos and articles that educate the general population on what is going on in the current real estate market. To do it right, you must let people in on what is going on in your life. Be the kind of person online that people want to be around offline. Let them feel like they know you so that when you do post something about your current property listings, people notice and pay attention. And as I learned from my good friend and mentor, Ray Higdon, *always* provide something of value to your followers. When done right, this is an extremely powerful tool that is *free*!

4. Signs and Banners

Putting signs and banners on your houses and in their front yards are a powerful and effective ways to get people calling about the house. I sell almost all my houses on lease-purchase programs, so when I post a sign or banner at my house, you can bet it is going to say, "Lease-Purchase! No-Bank Qualifying!" then of course I provide my phone number and website on the sign too.

5. Flyers

When I'm selling a house, I have my assistant find as many laundromats, pizza shops, grocery stores, or any place of business within a short distance of the house that will let us post flyers for that specific house. On that flyer, I have the little tabs at the bottom with my phone number on them so that people can take my information with them. It is also critical to have flyers available at your house, both inside and outside. I love to put an info box on or next to my yard signs. The flyers in those boxes have all the specs on that specific house, the terms on which it is available for purchase (price, lease purchase, owner financing, or whatever), and most importantly, I offer a buyer-referral fee of $500. The reason that is so critical is because people that live in any given neighborhood may want their friends and family to live nearby (well, in most cases that is true), but aren't willing to call the number on the sign or go inside and pick up in the info. That is why it is great to make it available so that people can just pull their car over, hop out, grab the sheet and be gone. We have all done this at least a few times, haven't we?

6. Realtors

There are several ways to use Realtors. You could list it with an agent, offer to pay 3% to any agent that brings you a buyer, or pay a flat-fee listing price. The price for a flat-fee listing is usually between $275 and $400, but why pay money upfront and risk not having it pay off? So, I have developed a relationship with a local agent where I pay him $600 to put the property in the MLS, but he only gets paid if and when the property gets sold. By the way, realtors have the same problem that loan officers do: they have people come to them that want to own a home but are not able to get one through traditional means. I will offer any agent that sends such a buyer to me anything from a $1,000 referral fee to a regular 3% commission. But I only pay the agent when I get paid, which in the case of a lease-option tenant-buyer, that means the realtor will get some money when they move into the house. But the majority of the commissions will be paid out if and when the tenant-buyer ends up purchasing the house.

7. Marketing Partners

Use the same strategies I listed in using marketing partners to find sellers… to find buyers. What you offer someone for sending you a buyer will vary greatly depending on what their expectations are and what their costs are, in finding the buyers, but regardless of the amount you pay for this, there is never any need for you to pay out any money for a lead (prospect) until you have made money from that prospect.

Wow! I just read through all the different ideas I gave you for marketing. That's a lot! Do you believe that it works? You should, because there isn't one strategy that I have given you that I and other investors all across the world have not personally implemented successfully.

There is one more question I have for you, and that is now that you have this information, *what are you going to do with it?* It is sad how many people I see go through the exact same real estate education that I have gone through, yet one or two years later, they still have not done their first deal. Does that sound familiar? Do you want to know the difference between the two people that sit side by side in the same seminar yet only one of them becomes a successful real estate investor? Is it the amount of time or money one has compared to the other? Does it have to do with background? Intelligence? I can assure you that it has nothing to do with any of them. Here is what it comes down to: implementation and determination. Of course there are other factors, but it all boils down to those two things. If you don't believe me, go ask another successful investor.

Friend, if you choose to become or already are a real estate investor, I sincerely want you to be successful. Now go out there and make it happen. You have plenty of tools readily available to you. If I, a twenty-three year old (former) landscaper can do it, surely anyone can!

Here's to your success!

Jim Zaspel

www.JimZaspel.com

ABOUT JIM

At the age of 23, Jim Zaspel has been in the real estate business for 18 months. One of Jim's passions is real estate – of course this most likely has to do with the fact that he made over $91,000 on just his second real estate deal!

Jim's entrepreneurial ventures did not begin with real estate; they began at the age of 12 when he started mowing neighbors' lawns with his dad's lawn mower. By the time he was 13 he had acquired 28 lawn accounts. This was more than he could do himself, so at the age of 13 he hired someone that was old enough to drive a pickup truck. After his family moved when he was 15, he sold the lawn care business. Over the next 7 years, he built up and sold 3 separate lawncare and landscaping companies, but he always knew that there was a better and more satisfying way to satisfy his entrepreneurial spirit. He found his answer in real estate at the age of 22.

After successfully investing in real estate for only one year, he was asked by Ron Le-Grand to become a mentor for his (Ron's) company to mentor new real estate investors and help them become successful as well. In addition to mentoring, Jim speaks at REIA (Real Estate Investor Association) meetings throughout the Philadelphia area, and is a member of Ron LeGrand's Mastermind group.

CHAPTER 9
THE 7 KEY INGREDIENTS THAT WILL ALLOW YOU TO NOT PARTICIPATE IN THE RECESSION

by Stephanie and Jon Iannotti

T hinking back to the time when Jon started as a Policeman in 1976, and more recently worked for the past 24 years in a Steel Mill in Butler, PA, and I worked 24 years as a Certified Orthopedic Technician and Personal Assistant to a Surgeon in Pittsburgh, little did we know that Real Estate Investing would provide us with the vehicle to leave our jobs, and make possible the lifestyle that we have today. Many of you probably have heard what a JOB is, right? (Just Over Broke!) Fortunately, the last 10 years of our lives have been in Real Estate Investing. It's not really about the Money…it's about the Freedom. Our story will tell you that we refuse to participate in the current Economic Recession and if we can do it….<u>YOU CAN TOO</u>!

Fortunes are created from chaos and we definitely subscribe to that theory! When everyone is running and hiding or sticking their heads in the sand, we are doing more and more business than ever! Why? And how?... you may ask.

Well, here are the "7 Key Ingredients":-

The First Ingredient: "PRIVATE MONEY." Real Estate Investing is so much fun when you have the CA$H to work with. Once we mastered the art of getting Private Money Mortgages, the doors were unlocked. Helping people in this recession to make money with their Savings, IRA's and 401k's is mutually rewarding. It is amazing once you show them how to make money, they then also tell their friends and your private money sources continue to grow.

TIP: Here is the biggest tip we can give you to help you in your quest to obtain private money. Ask your potential investor this simple question..."Do you currently have an IRA or other investment capital that is not making you a good rate of return?" When they say yes...you know you have a very good potential private money candidate. If they say no, take it one step further, ask them if they know of anyone that may have an IRA or other investment capital that is not giving them a good rate of return. Always try to get a referral if they themselves don't have the money to invest.

Also, one more bonus tip, *don't ever assume people have or don't have money to invest*. Ask everyone you know if they would be interested in earning a good rate of return on their money, secured by Real Estate. Believe us when we tell you that you will be surprised by the fact that people you think have the money don't, and people you think don't have the money, do.

Private money is a very vital, important part of our Business!

The Second Ingredient: "YOUR POWER TEAM." This is a major key to our success. It starts with your Attorney. You need a Real Estate Attorney that actually "gets it" when it comes to Creative Real Estate Investing.

TIP: Go to your local REIA (Real Estate Investment Association) and find out which Attorney most of the big Investors are using and that more than likely will be your Power Team Attorney! Many times these Attorneys are very active in the REIA and may also give discounts to the members that use their services.

You need a Real Estate Attorney who understands the creative ways of how we do business, and preferably one that is doing deals themselves, as this keeps their skills sharp.

You will also need a Realtor who really understands Real Estate Investing; again, one that is doing business themselves is usually your best bet. They have to be able to think like you do, so that they can present the right offers for you and prescreen the properties for you. Realtors are a great source for your CMA's (Comparative Market Analysis) that you will need for all prospects and properties. You will also need the Realtor to place offers on any properties listed on the MLS, and to place multiple offers on the Bank-owned properties, most commonly called REO's (Real Estate Owned).

TIP: Interview your Realtor....ask them questions about Real Estate Investing and let them know that you are a CA$H BUYER....! Again, many times you will find your best Realtors at the local REIA, as they are on top of Investor's needs and are many times Investors themselves.

Next on the team is a great "LOAN BROKER"....You will want a Broker that has a visible track record of getting buyers financed. Your broker needs to have access to many different loan products, such as FHA, VA, USDA, and Conventional Loans.

TIP: Ask your Loan Broker how many loans they process per month and how many closings they have. This will allow you to be able to tell if they are really doing the business and if their loan products suit the majority of buyers today.

Next is your "Personal Assistant"...This has to be someone very proficient, someone that you can delegate to, and also be able to 'take the ball and run with it.' Someone that is a 'quick study', is able to help you follow thru' on your plans, someone that will think like you, and is able to make good decisions.

TIP: When you interview a "Personal Assistant," look for the one that asks you what they can do to help you move your business to the next level....not what you are going to do for them! If they are more concerned about helping you achieve your goals, they obviously get the fact that if you accomplish your goals, and they are a vital part in that achievement, then they will be rewarded well. A bit of advice is <u>to</u>

<u>make sure that you make it worth their while</u> to be such an important part of your team!

One of the biggest changes we underwent in our business about 14 months ago was to hire two VA's (Virtual Assistants). We can honestly say that this changed our business for the better. Our Virtual Assistants again gave us the ability to work from another state and continue to do business across the country. This also allows us not to have the costs of a physical office - for everyone works from home. One of our VA's lives in Florida and one in Texas and anyone calling into our virtual office would never know that they are not sitting in our office!

Our VA's do our website updates, answering of phones, email blasts, voice mail blasts, giving out lock box codes to potential buyers, spreadsheets, buyers lists, property information sheets, updating property flyers and many, many other duties. They are an invaluable part of our business, as they are the ones to whom many of the duties are delegated.

TIP: Make sure you go through a reputable company to hire your VA as it will save you time and money.

Another very important part of our team is our "Acquisitionist." This is an important part of our business as this person talks to the prospective seller, they get the numbers together for the deal, take pictures, video and then presents the property to us. Once a decision is made to purchase the property, they do the contracts, meet the seller, and get the seller to closing. Once closed, the Acquisitionist may also help with the management of the rehab project if the property needs some renovation. We can tell you that our Acquisitionist has had some 'pretty fun' experiences and has seen some 'pretty amazing' things when it comes to Sellers and Houses. She has been chased by bats, stepped in many a 'pile of poop', and handled many sellers that just didn't know which way to go.

TIP: Finding a good Acquisitionist is vital, as they will be the one that will be communicating with the sellers. They must be able to efficiently present offers and must really have a very well-rounded Real Estate Investing knowledge. This is the person that will be your physical representative, so make sure they look, act and present well.

Another very important part of our team is our Loan Coordinator.

This person plays a critical part in keeping your buyers' loans running smoothly. The loan coordinator takes the original application, and gets it to the Broker. Then they work closely with the Broker to keep the buyers moving smoothly and swiftly to closing. Our loan coordinator is also the one who coordinates the closing and attends the closing, thus making sure that everything is in place, and is there to assist the Broker, the Attorney and the Buyer, ensuring a smooth closing.

TIP: Our Loan Coordinator is also the one that signs for us at the closing - via a corporate resolution that allows her to act as a corporate officer. She then makes copies of the closing check and deposits the funds into our bank, thus allowing us never to have to attend closings.

We certainly can't forget the Bookkeeper and CPA. These are usually two separate people but not always. In our Team we have both a Book-keeper and a CPA. Both are very vital to the team, as they are the ones that keep our finances in place. They are responsible for keeping every-thing straight for our business partner…. "Uncle Sam."

TIP: Your bookkeeper should provide you with monthly reports to show where you are in your business. Your CPA should provide you with advice to keep your taxes minimized and your earnings maximized! An added bonus would be a CPA that is also a Real Estate Investor. They are more inclined to keep up with all the changes and deductions in the business. Again, your REIA is a great place to find this crucial part of your team!

The Third Ingredient: In today's economy we have found that auto-mation and systematization are not only 'key' to doing our deals, but to free us up to do other things in our business that generate more income streams… such as Bulk REO's, Mentoring locally and Internationally, and an MLM or two for additional passive income.

By putting our businesses in Pennsylvania on "Cruise Control" with our systems and automation, we are able to now live in SW Florida. We continue to do business in PA and across the country by leveraging systems and other people. We like to say that 98% of our business can be done by Phone, Fax, FedEx, and e-mail.

The Fourth Ingredient: We enjoy Partnering and Joint Venturing, of-ten called JV, with other investors across the country as this allows us to again leverage our time and efforts. If the numbers make sense, and someone is looking for guidance on a deal, we partner on it and everyone WINS. These are our favorite kinds of deals...when we can help someone that doesn't really know how to structure the deal, and we all win by working together and accomplishing the common goal. Mentoring is in our hearts and we truly love to give back to others, as knowledge is a major part of the success in Real Estate Investing.

The Fifth Ingredient: Another very important part of our business in today's economy is Online Marketing and Social Media. This is becoming a huge part of our business not only to sell properties but in many other aspects as well. The networking connections have become priceless to our business! We have connections for Funding, Bulk REO's, Platforms, Sellers, Buyers, Joint Venture Partners, and for many other business leaders across the country. This method of connecting is becoming a major focus for our business.

TIP: If you are not involved in Social Networking and Online Marketing, you are missing out on a big part of your potential business and success!

The Sixth Ingredient: Creative Financing. You know, when the masses are going in one direction, the ones making the most money are the ones going in the opposite direction. Ron LeGrand always told us, "The Money is in the Paper." Banks are selling off their notes and mortgages. They are all doing it! Mortgages are harder and harder to obtain in today's economy...so, we decided... "Let's go the opposite direction." Let's create mortgages and notes and sell our properties with Seller Financing. We have now become the bank! After all why not make the interest on these homes instead of the Banks! In fact, think about it, the Banks had all the big beautiful buildings, even before we gave them billions in tax money.

So on a typical deal we would normally make $25,000. The lender would finance the buyer for us, and make over $144,000 on a typical 30 year loan of say $125,000 at 6% interest. So we switched to Owner Financing for our Buyers on some of our properties, and now we are the Bank and making all the interest on the loan, not the banks...because we are now the Bank!

The Seventh Ingredient: Last but certainly not least, do everything with Integrity, Gratitude and Compassion. Remember.... "Do Unto Others as You Would Have Them Do Unto You." We are all in this world to help each other. If you always keep this motto in your heart and in your business, it will help you achieve all of your goals. Just remember that someone's loss will sometimes be someone's gain, as that's how the world works, unfortunately. Always remember that you should never take advantage of someone that can be helped. In other words.... do the right thing! If someone can be helped to keep their home...Help them. If you can provide a service that most people charge for and you are in a position not to charge...take that opportunity to help others. It will come back to you tenfold and sometimes more. Be grateful for all that you have, and show compassion to others, as not everyone is as fortunate as we are. Light a warm flame in all the people's hearts that you touch. We can't tell you how many people have told us that they sincerely appreciate us for helping them either buy a home or help them out of a bad situation with a current home. This is what it's all about, and yes, along the way we do make money. After all, it is a business, but it is a people business first and foremost!

TIP: Remember, your company is only as good as the people that are running it! One thing we learned that could help you in your business is HIRE SLOW and FIRE FAST. When you own and operate a business from another state, you have to be able to trust and rely on the people that are working for you...so take your time and find the right people.

To sum up the <u>Seven Keys to Our Success</u> that has kept us from participating in the current recession. They are:

1. Private Money eliminates the banks and gives us a huge pool of funds to use for deals, thus allowing us to be CA$H BUYERS and close quickly. Remember CA$H IS ALWAYS KING in the Real Estate Investing Arena.
2. Our power team assists us in all the processes of the business.
3. Our systems and automation streamline the business to allow us to focus on the other income streams.
4. The Internet has opened up the world to us to do deals ANY- WHERE. It allows us to partner and JV as needed.
5. Networking connections through online Marketing and Social Media have become vital to our success.
6. Creative financing not only gives us the EXIT strategy of choice

to sell properties, but also the Cash Stream that the banks have enjoyed for years!

and finally,

7. Integrity, Gratitude and Compassion will be the fuel that will keep your business fire lit for many, many years if you always keep them at the top of your Business Motto.

One Final TIP: If you are thinking that now is a BAD time to get into Real Estate Investing...think again! There will be more millionaires made in Real Estate Investing in the next couple years than there probably have been in the last 20 years combined...! You may ask how....? Leverage, Timing, Banking Chaos, Mortgage Chaos, all equal Huge Success if you know what to do with all the Chaos. *Our biggest piece of advice if you are really interested in becoming very wealthy using Real Estate as your vehicle....get a good Mentor that is actively involved in the business.* Let them guide you, as it will sharply diminish your learning curve and will allow you to cut the time to your success dramatically. Think about it...who do you know that is really, really successful that does not have a Mentor? The cost of a good Mentor might seem high...but we can guarantee you that the cost of NO Mentor would be much higher!

To Your Abundance and Success!!

Stephanie and Jon Iannotti

ABOUT STEPHANIE AND JON

The Iannotti's have successfully bought and sold hundreds of single family, multi-family and commercial properties. They have also trained and partnered with over 75 of their students in Real Estate through their Real Estate Investing Mentorship Program. The Iannotti's invest with their student partners anywhere in the U.S. and are International Mentors for Ron LeGrand's Millionaire Mentorship Program.

Stephanie and Jon currently own and operate 4 successful businesses in Pennsylvania and Florida and have been speakers at numerous Investing events. If you are interested in learning more about their group or would like to have them speak at one of your organizations, please feel free to email them at: butlerswebuyhouses@earthlink.net or contact their office at 724-283-5021 ext # 3 and ask for Julie. The Iannotti's feel that the next 2 years are what they are calling "THE PERFECT STORM" for Real Estate Investing across the country.

Real Estate Investing has worked well for them as they have been self employed for the last 7 years and loving every minute of their entrepreneurial lives.

www.Thelannottis.com

CHAPTER 10
MASTERING THE NEW MARKET. HOW TO GET YOUR PIECE OF THE BAILOUT.

by Lisa Donner

Why Buy and Hold still works with multi-family properties, and how you can get the government help pay you to do it!

A s a real estate investor, I love to get paid to buy, rehab, hold and sell real estate. If done correctly, you can make a profit at each stage and it's a great way to make money, especially in the market we have today. And what a market! As you know, the real estate market has taken a huge hit in pricing and foreclosures are at an all-time high. This has created a situation where banks have a lot of property on their hands, and they want to get rid of it quickly.

This overload, which is known as REO (Real Estate Owned) by banks, has created a unique opportunity for the savvy investor. It is a rare opportunity and I want to show you how to take advantage of it in the current economic climate.

AN UNTAPPED REVENUE SOURCE: MULTI-FAMILY PROPERTIES

Multi-family units are the secret to your success. This includes duplexes, triplexes and fourplexes. Why multi-family properties instead of single family? It's a simple case of math, really. If you are building a portfolio of properties, single family dwellings offer little to no steady cash flow, even when rented. And when they're empty, you end up losing a month or more of rental income, reducing your cash flow further.

I think you'll understand the advantages of multi-family properties if I use my own personal experience as an example.

I recently purchased a duplex that had two 1,100 square-foot units with 3-bedrooms, 2 baths and a 2 car garage each. The duplex was built in 2003 and last sold in August 2006 for $298,000. When the bottom fell out of the market rental, rates at the duplex inevitably went down, and the owner lost the property in foreclosure.

Three years later I purchased the property for – are you ready? Are you sure? Would you believe just $40,000! That's right, $40,000! I'm not making this up. Why was it so cheap? A lot of investors won't touch a multi-family property because it takes too long to flip and they can't get the return on the investment they want, so they stick with single family residences.

As a real estate investor I knew this, and armed with that knowledge, realized that the competition in the REO world wasn't as stiff for this type of property. So I could get a multi-family for a much lower buy in.

USING OTHER PEOPLE'S MONEY

Best of all, I could purchase my duplex with other people's money so my own money wasn't tied up. Believe it or not, there are private lenders out there who are ready to make money in the current real estate market, but they either don't have the time to learn or don't want to play the real estate game.

I ended up borrowing $70,000 and gave the lender a first mortgage, a signed promissory note, title insurance and listed them as an additional insured on the insurance policy.

How did the deal work out numbers-wise? The math is pretty basic:

$70,000 private lender
- $40,000 purchase price
- $3,000 closing costs
- $4,000 holding costs
$15,000 rehab costs
$ 8,000 acquisition fee

The $70,000 covered all the costs of the acquisition and rehab. It also left an "acquisition fee" of $8,000. Remember when I talked about getting paid to buy, hold and rehab property? That $8,000 went directly to me!

USING THE GOVERNMENT'S MONEY

Of course, a private lender is just one borrowing strategy for multi-family properties. You can also use your county's HUD program. They have so much money to lend, they don't even know about it. In fact, chances are good they'll initially tell you that they don't have any programs for you. In most parts of the country, that's not true! Don't let them convince you of this. Be persistent and tell them that you know there is some kind of program to help landlords rehab property.

Since this is the government you're dealing with, know ahead of time that the going will be slow, very slow, the first time you do this. But ask them about Block Grants in your area and find out who administers them. Once you've found the right department, become their best friend. They have the power to give you money... lots and lots of FREE money. But you'll have to be persistent and patient.

I have used this before where I live. My county calls their program "Rental Rehab." To gain access to these funds, I had to fill out a 10-page application and hand over a $100 application fee. A week later, I was approved and the rehab wheels began to turn.

FOLLOWING THE RULES

At this point, it was time for the inspector to enter the picture. It's the county inspector's job to see what needs to be done to the property. The county was ready to invest $10,000 in the rehab project, based on the fact that it was a 3-bedroom home. Since there were two 3-bedroom homes in the duplex, each unit received $10,000 for a total of $20,000.

This money isn't without strings. But they're not insurmountable. Here were the particular requirements for this project:

- The property can be rented to anyone, but it must be made available to low-income Section 8 tenants as well.
- If a tenant was already in place, I couldn't require them to leave.
- Everything must be up to code.

That was it. Oh, and I would also have to kick in some of my own dough. Unlike a private investor who may be willing to invest 100% of the funds needed, government programs want you to assume some of the risk as well.

GOING THROUGH REHAB

I know this sounds confusing, so let me illustrate it for you.

Say a duplex cost a total of $35,000 to rehab. The county portion was $20,000. You have to put up $10,000 (1/3 of the $30,000 total funded for the rehab under county rules) plus the additional $5,000 that wasn't covered. You don't actually get any money from the county. You pay the contractor your portion first and then the contractor bills the county for the balance, up to the $20,000 they agreed to pay. Notice, the county is paying you $20,000 to rehab your property – money you don't have to find on your own.

Once the inspector looks at the property, it takes about three to four weeks to receive the itemized list of all the repairs that need to be done. If the cost is beyond your budget, eliminate things that don't specifically relate to the building code.

If these are improvements you still need to make, you can always find another source of funding. For example, after this project was completed I learned that there is a weatherization program available for homeowners and landlords. The program will pay up to $5,000 per unit for things like air conditioning, windows, doors, weather stripping, etc. If I had known this before I did this duplex, I would have had the doors and A/C done through this program and gotten them for free.

Armed with the list of repairs and the cost estimate, it's time to shop for a General Contractor who can look over the specs and give you a bid. Don't let him see the estimates you have and be sure to get bids from at least three contractors. If you want to save some time use General Contractors that are already registered through the same county program. Otherwise, you may have to wait three weeks or more to get them through the approval process.

Now that you have your bids and you, your contractor and the county are all on the same page, you're ready for the next step. As I said, the money is free, but it's not really free. This is the government's money, after all, and they just don't hand it over to you. Once this project was completely approved, I had a General Contractor ready to go and I could show the county I had my portion of the funds, we were ready to sign the papers. The county had already performed a title check as with a normal closing.

For me to get the county's portion I had to sign mortgage documents for a 10-year, self-amortizing 0% interest, zero payment loan. This is supposed to keep the property from being sold before the 10-year period is over. But if you need to sell it, you just have to pay back the unused portion. Note: You don't want to do this too often or they will no longer loan you funds. But if you can work within the requirements, this is a great deal.

For my duplex, some basic repairs needed to be done. This meant all new interior and exterior doors, new paint inside and out, removal of the carpet and installation of 18" tile throughout, new countertops and appliances, replacement of the A/C unit, repair of the well, a poured concrete driveway and walkways to replace the gravel ones, servicing and cleaning of all systems, and a general cleaning inside and out from top to bottom. The contractor finished the entire rehab in a little more than a month.

The property is absolutely gorgeous. Looking all shiny and new, it was so much easier to rent now. But that's the property manager's job, not mine. Now the property rents for $675 per side, bringing in $1,350 per month. The funds I borrowed from my private lender are amortized at 8% over 30 years and the monthly payments are $515 per month. Once I factor in the taxes, insurance, maintenance and vacancy contingencies, I'm left with a positive cash flow of $400 per month.

BUY. HOLD. REHAB. REPEAT.

Let's review this project for a moment. The 2003 duplex was originally worth $298,000. I paid $40,000 to purchase it and an additional $22,000 to bring it up to "like new" condition. The replacement cost of this place is valued at $160,000.

I got paid $8,000 to buy the building, picked up another $20,000 from the county for rehab, currently receive $400 a month to hold the duplex, and stand to make $98,000 if I sell it, though I don't plan to do that anytime soon.

Imagine repeating this strategy over and over. See how multi-family properties can be so profitable? All you need is to find the right property, work the numbers and follow the steps outlined above. Don't feel limited to just duplexes. Once you have a duplex or two under your belt, venture into triplexes and fourplexes for even more revenue generating possibilities.

GETTING STARTED

Thanks to the housing meltdown, these residential properties are there for the taking. Since they are smaller multi-family properties, they don't attract a lot of attention, either from those seeking to flip single-family homes or those interested in larger complexes.

Use the MLS listings to find your target properties and then do your homework so you can make a smart offer. Go after the ones that have been listed for a long time and at a slightly higher price than you want to pay. As the end of the quarter approaches, banks are often willing to accept a lower offer to get the property off the books to bolster their sagging bottom lines.

Whatever you do, don't be afraid of the new market. More millionaires are made in a time of chaos than at any other time. Get out there and get your feet wet in some multi-family real estate and see for yourself how easy it is to get paid to buy, rehab, hold and sell property.

And if you need help, visit us at our website: www.SWFLRealEstate-Coach.com we'd love to talk with you. We'll be happy to give you a free report and free consultation to help you realize your dreams.

ABOUT LISA

Rick and Lisa Donner's story starts out pretty normal. Rick is originally from western Pennsylvania, and Lisa is from Miami. Rick is a CPA in Fort Myers, FL with a practice that has a concentration in real estate investing. Lisa has been an entrepreneur and has owned and managed several businesses. She began a women's real estate investing group in April 2007 which has an average attendance of 50.

Rick and Lisa have successfully bought and sold numerous properties over the last several years helping both those who need to sell and those who want to buy. They currently focus on quick turning single family houses and holding multi-family and commercial properties. As Real Estate Coaches and Mentors, Rick and Lisa teach their students how to become successful real estate investors using various techniques and strategies based on current market conditions. In other words, what's working now and how you can apply it to make money. The Donners are also Mentors for Ron LeGrand's Millionaire Mentorship Program, having students both throughout the U.S. and internationally. As believers in multiple streams of income, they have several successful businesses in addition to their Real Estate Investing and CPA businesses.

To learn more about The Donners, and discover how you can Make Money in Real Estate RIGHT NOW and receive a FREE Special Report entitled "Learn 4 Money-Making Strategies To Make Money Now," visit: www.SWFLRealEstateCoach.com or call Toll Free 1-888-548-8450.

www.SWFLRealEstateCoach.com

CHAPTER 11
MAKING MONEY ON A SHOESTRING BUDGET IN ANY MARKET, USA

A NON-TRADITIONAL APPROACH TO REOS

by Matt and Rich McLean

When we first became interested in real estate we could barely spell real estate. Thus we began by getting bank loans to buy, remodel and sell houses. We had some mild success until things like "sub prime," "mortgage meltdown" and "lending crisis" started to make the headlines and foreclosures flooded the market. Anytime banks were involved problems arose. Investors could not get loans to buy and rehab houses, and owner occupants could not get loans to buy these newly fixed up homes because of the bank's tightening credit requirements and waning lending power. They say it will get worse in 2010 before it gets better. Fortunately, amidst the chaos, we discovered how to avoid banks altogether unless by choice. We choose to help liquidate their REO inventory.

Most investors in today's market have heard of REO properties even if they do not fully understand what that means. Simply put, REO or "real estate owned" is the term given to a piece of property that goes back to the bank after an unsuccessful foreclosure auction. The REO becomes a liability to the bank because it is not producing income and it limits the bank's lending power. Banks do not want liabilities, but they are getting them in record numbers.

In our East Tennessee region, the Chamber of Commerce says we are a "diversified and stable market" that has not experienced any major bubbles or busts. In the areas with high foreclosure rates, there is more REO inventory and generally more opportunities to buy cheap real estate. Even with that being the case, there are still plenty of REO bargains and less competition in stable markets across the USA.

We wanted to take advantage of the Buyer's market. Our initial hesitation to get in was based in the fear of not being able to: 1) find a bargain, 2) get the money to take the plunge, and 3) sell the property. In this chapter we are not only going to share with you how you can identify a bargain REO, but also how to buy it on a shoestring budget. Then, we are then going to show you how to sell that property quickly without doing any repairs and receive quick cash now. Finally, we will illustrate how to hold a property and receive cash now, cash flow and cash later without the use of banks or any of your own funds. Some of these methods are non-traditional but are powerful tools that can be used in any market in the USA. We used three examples of our recent deals to illustrate our journey in learning about these tools.

JOHNSON AVENUE

The REO property on Johnson Avenue was a four bedroom, two bath, two story, 1800 square foot frame house that needed about $30,000 in repairs and was listed at $25,800. As a side note, one of the benefits of buying REO's is that banks are not emotionally attached to their houses, so you only have to deal with making the math work. Considering the math, we had two choices to determine value, which is the basis for determining if a house is a bargain:

MAO Formula: ARV (after repair value) X 65% - repairs= MAO (maximum allowable offer). Never pay MAO.

Street Formula: Determine what CASH buyers are paying for houses in similar condition in this area and buy it for less.

The MAO formula requires that you estimate the cost of repairs and determine the value of the repaired property. We learned a shortcut for estimating repairs from one of our mentors, Cameron Dunlap. By categorizing the repairs as "bad," ""really bad," or "awful," you can quickly determine general repair costs if you know the square feet of the house. "Bad" is a general makeover with no major repairs ($10/sq ft). "Really bad" is a general makeover plus one or two majors like new roof and windows ($15/sq ft). "Awful" is a total rehab with structural damage, missing plumbing, HVAC, sagging roof, etc. ($20/sq ft). You may need to adjust your square foot pricing, but this general rule gets it pretty close. Just know that every house is going to need some repairs, no matter what the condition of the house. Always assign a minimum of $5,000 worth of repairs to a house, even if it only needs to be cleaned. There are always surprises and Murphy lives in your town, we promise.

Estimating the value of a property can be done by gathering comparable sales or "comps" from that subject neighborhood. Comps can be obtained from several online services. Some of these services are free and some you pay for but you usually get what you pay for. You must be careful to get recent sales and compare apples to apples.

The Street Formula requires you to determine what cash buyers are paying for properties in a particular neighborhood. The MLS is the best source to obtain information on areas in which cash is being used to buy houses and in what quantities. Since Realtors have the keys to the MLS and the REO vault, you need to team up with a Realtor to gain MLS access and to get to the REO listings. We cannot stress enough the importance of building relationships with Realtors.

We decided that we wanted to wholesale the Johnson Ave property to a cash buyer and not do any repairs. Therefore, we needed to verify the price cash buyers were paying for these properties. The MLS data indicated that cash buyers were paying $30,000-$35,000 for this type of house in this particular area. This confirmed our MAO calculated as follows: ARV= $100,000, Repairs= $30,000; (100,000 x 0.65 – 30,000 = 35,000). Most cash buyers are paying close to MAO. Our goal was to make a minimum of $6,000 and not put more than $1000 of our own money into the deal. This strategy would result in minimum cash output and quick cash now. If you don't have funds for the earnest money deposit, partner with someone who does on your first deal and give them a percentage of the profit. Remember, those who have the gold make the rules, so it may have to be a 50/50 split or greater. That's OK because the important thing is to make the deal happen, get a paycheck and build your confidence.

When submitting an offer to a Realtor, it is important to have a contract with no contingencies, no inspection period, and POF (proof of funds) for a CASH sale in order to be competitive. If you do not have POF, then use a friend, family member or an investor to supply this to you and give them a small percentage of the profit at closing. Again, a little bit of something is better than a whole lot of nothing. Our offer was $24,000 since we assumed we could sell it for about $30,000. The offer was made the day the house came on the market, was one of several received and it was not the highest offer. However, because it had no inspection periods or contingencies and it was for cash, it was accepted. As you can see, our offer was very close to the asking price. However, do not let the asking price determine what you are going to offer. Base your offer on the formulas and your exit strategy.

We set the closing date for 30 days after the contract was signed and set out to find a buyer. As Ron LeGrand has taught us, the best way to find a buyer is to put out 20 ugly hand written signs in the area advertising a "must sell" house. The sign said **"House – 4/2 1800 sq ft – Handyman special – CASH"** and a phone number. Over a two week period we received over 100 calls. We gave the qualified buyers the lock box code and they inspected the house on their schedule. We never went back to the house. Even though we were targeting investors, we signed a contract with someone who wanted to live there and could do their own repairs. We sold the house to them for $33,000. As a bonus, we developed a good cash buyer's list and put it to use as we immediately sold another REO property the same way, without advertising. Because we bought the Johnson Ave house at a price to sell to investors, but ended up selling to a homeowner, we were able to increase our profit from $6,000 to $9,000.

The non-conventional method in this transaction came at the closing. In order not to use more than $1000 (required earnest money- sometimes as little as $500) we had to find a buyer for it before we closed. Since

Banks will not let you assign an REO contract to another buyer, you must close on the house before you sell it. In other words, our buyer would have to buy the house from us *after* we closed on it but *before* we had to write a check to our seller. Buying the house does not mean you must put out your own cash. If you can sell the house within minutes after you buy it, and your buyer's cash is in escrow at the closing agent's office, then your buyer's cash is wired to the bank selling the REO as well as paying you. Timing is everything and these details must be clearly disclosed to your buyer in the Purchase and Sales Agreement. Since all of these details were in order we went to closing having deposited only $1,000 for the earnest money and left with a $9,000 profit. By the way, our contract with our buyer was $33,000 "Net to Seller." They paid for all closing costs.

In summary, the Johnson house is one example of using readily available resources, cheap advertising, and creative but legal closing techniques to buy a house on a shoestring budget anywhere in the USA. This house produced cash now but no cash flow or cash later. Our next example gave us all three, but we almost got more than we bargained for.

KYLE AVENUE

By the beginning of 2008, even though the market was declining, we were naïve enough to try to buy, fix and sell a house with conventional lending. Since we had used this approach before, we went to a bank based on 30 years of good credit, a free and clear house and a promise of our 'first born' child. We secured funds for the purchase and rehab of an REO on Kyle Ave. This three bedroom one-bath house for $38,000 had good potential; it just needed about 20K worth of rehab. Initial comps put the ARV at $100,000. Rehab and holding costs put our costs of the house at $60,000. We went to work selling the property on the MLS with our realtor. After six months and a significant price drop, our listing expired and we had nothing but debt and a headache. The market had come to a screeching halt and no one was buying because the banks were not lending. What now?

We were just starting to pay attention to Ron LeGrand during this time and he said that not only could we sell in this market environment but that we could obtain the happy trinity of cash now, cash flow and cash later. We thought he was full of crap, but we didn't have a better plan.

We put the biggest, ugliest sign you have ever seen in the front yard. We used a full sheet of plywood, painted it orange, and said "HOUSE FOR SALE, NO BANK QUALIFYING" and a phone number. Additionally, we put out 20 bandit signs that pointed to the house in a 5 block radius. We put applications in the house, directed all the calls to a 24 hour voice message center that told them what the lock box code was and how to leave a message. We never showed the house, and only talked to buyers that were motivated enough to follow our instructions. Finally, a qualified buyer came forth to lease the house with the option to buy it for $105,000, gave a $5,000 down payment and netted us a sweet cash flow. What about the bank loan?

Ron told us about using private money. He said we should have used this from the very beginning and avoided the banks like the plague. Banks wanted their money every month; we needed to keep it every month. As we talked to people about our real estate investing we learned that some of them would like to get involved but did not know how. So, we invited two people to invest. Their combined investment yielded a 60 percent LTV (loan to value) ratio. They received a promissory note secured by a Deed of Trust on the Kyle Ave house and we paid for all the closing costs, including Lender title and fire insurance policies. Even if we had bad credit, they would have invested, based on the low level of risk and high rate of return. We refinanced Kyle Ave using our new private funds and got the bank out of our lives. Therefore, we eliminated our liability, monthly payment requirements and saved our firstborn.

We almost got caught in the market downturn with a house that was going nowhere with us trying to sell to those who must use banks. However, we now have two happy investors who have deferred their interest payment until we cash out the house and a tenant who is looking forward to owning the house in another year. Cash now, cash flow, and cash later. Thank you Ron Legrand.

BRADFORD STREET

After the Kyle Ave and Johnson Ave houses, we wanted to leverage our time and money even further. We wanted to stretch our thinking further outside the box and we didn't want to put a dime of our money into our next deal. We honed in on our experimental subject, the REO market. The house on Bradford Street was a four bedroom, two bath, two story,

1700 sq-ft brick and frame foreclosure. It was in better repair than the previous examples but was priced at $60,300. On the outside it looked like it was ready to move in. However, on the inside there was a collapsed ceiling and two damaged walls from a water leak. The unknown cause of the leak was keeping buyers away. Since the house condition was no worse than bad, we estimated the repair at about $15,000 (about $10 per sq-ft). We wanted to buy, repair, and lease option this house to produce cash now, a cash flow and cash later when our tenant got their own financing.

In order to determine what we were willing to pay for the house we calculated MAO as follows: ARV=$120,000; repairs=$15,000; (120,000 x 0.65 - 15,000 = 63,000). Typically, cash buyers will pay close to MAO. However, the Street Formula told us cash buyers were paying between $45,000- $55,000. In order for us to leave the wholesale option open (always buy with multiple exit strategies in mind), we needed to try to buy the Bradford property below or at the bottom of this range which was well below MAO. We wrote a contract for $45,000 that was rejected by the bank. However, the realtor knew we were serious and offered to let us know if the asking price was reduced. The bank ended up dropping the price of the house and we again offered $45,000 and settled at $46,100.00.

We advertised this house, with signs and the internet, as a cash purchase and as a lease to own property simultaneously. We wanted to test the accuracy of the Street Formula and simultaneously continue to build our cash buyer's list. The accuracy of the Street Formula was confirmed when we received multiple calls but no offers at our $56,000 cash price. We probably could have sold the house for $52,000, making an easy $5000 and moved on to the next deal. Even though that is not a lot of money for a wholesale deal, it may be the oxygen you need to keep your suffocating business alive. If so, cash now is a good and beautiful thing. But what if you could make a quick $5,000-$10,000 now, create a $500-$1000 per month cash flow, not make any monthly payments, not use any of your own money and receive a substantial check at a later date? Sound too good? We thought so too. Here's how we did it.

First, we offered an investor (someone that we already knew) the chance to make a high rate of return with his money secured by real property at a loan to value ratio of less than 60%. In addition, we introduced him to the concept of using a self directed IRA to invest in real estate notes. He could either defer paying taxes on his return using a traditional IRA or grow the investment tax free investing with a Roth IRA. We quickly had $65,000 to work with and bought the house, fixed the plumbing leak, repaired the ceiling and walls, made some minor repairs and placed a lease option tenant in the house with $5,000 down, $800 per month and a contract to buy the house in 24 months for $104,900 provided that he improve the house over the next 12 months. This contract is very specific as to what is to be done and by what time. Since a mortgage broker determined that our tenant could buy the house in 18 months, our buyer has a six-month cushion to get a refinance loan to cash us out of the property. With all of our lease option tenants, the maintenance of the house is their responsibility. It turned out that the tenant is a licensed contractor with all the skills needed to make the house reach its full potential. This tenant is trading sweat for equity, thus a good example of a sweat equity lease option.

In this example we did not use any of our own money, received cash when we bought the house, have a net cash flow of about $600 per month after taxes and insurance, and have a tenant that will raise the value of the house to its full potential. This is cash now, cash flow and cash later at it's finest with no money out of our pocket and we are selling in this market. Sweet!

These examples occurred in a mid-sized college town in Tennessee where there was never a big bubble and life just ambles along. It is not a hot market and the banks are very conservative. These methods are somewhat unconventional for our town and probably yours too. However, using these methods appropriately, we can almost guarantee that they will help you achieve your goals of obtaining cash now, cash flow and cash later anywhere there are REOs in America, which is everywhere. Good hunting.

ABOUT MATT AND RICHARD

Matt McLean started his professional career as an athletic trainer taking care of people such as Peyton Manning at the University of Tennessee. His scholarship earned him national awards as a student athletic trainer and he enjoyed the fruits of being part of the 1998 National Football Championship staff. His love for real estate began seven years ago in a hot market in Asheville, NC when he wholesaled a house and made $13,000 in a week. He hasn't looked back since. Training under Ron LeGrand has made a rank amateur into a professional that has a wealth of tools to take advantage of this exciting market. He is constantly teaching and encouraging other investors as well as giving hope to those trying to get their families back under a roof that belongs to them. The techniques that are outlined in this chapter are just some examples of those available to Ron LeGrand's students. Matt's goal is to continue demonstrating excellence in his work by being a successful investor, great husband and dad of three, and helping to heal some of what is broken in his community.

Growing up in Daytona Beach, Florida immersed Richard McLean in seawater early in life. His passion for sea creatures and for sports came together at Florida State University where he played football, ran track and acquired a Ph. D. in marine biology. A career in marine research and environmental assessment has taken him from the warm seas of the South Pacific to the frozen seas of Antarctica. Having an expertise in shallow water environments resulted in being part of the Cousteau team that filmed **"The Incredible March of the Spiny Lobsters"** for the **Undersea World of Jacque Cousteau** television series. In addition, he was the technical advisor for the BBC's **Blue Planet Series, "The Tidal Seas"** that showcased some of Dr. McLean's research. Currently, the building of wetlands has dominated his scientific endeavors. However, developing a real estate expertise with his son Matt has evolved from a hobby to a serious business during the last seven years. Under the teaching of Ron LeGrand and his mentoring program, he has put his training to work to learn the science and art of real estate investing in any market in the United States. He has bought and sold properties in three states and is now concentrating on Tennessee where the techniques in the chapter coauthored with Matt are being successfully used to build a business that is worth writing about.

CHAPTER 12
SECRETS TO PROFITING FROM REAL ESTATE IN ANY ECONOMY

by Nathan Witt

I n the new economy too much time is spent listening to, speaking of and thinking about the 'doom and gloom' of our real estate market. National and local media bombard us with story after story of the sub-prime mortgage meltdown, plummeting market values, overleveraged homeowners, skyrocketing foreclosure rates, tight lending practices, ...and on, ...and on, ...and on. Here's the thing, as real estate entrepreneurs, we have a choice. Either we buy-in to the 'doom and gloom', curl up in our respective corners and wait for the market correction to complete its course, or we can act like true entrepreneurs and seek out the new opportunities that inevitably present themselves during chaotic times.

Rather than participating in a faltering economy, why not actively seek to profit from it? When we do, we not only take a path that leads to financial prosperity, but we also position ourselves to help others out of what may be their most challenging financial times. Creating 'win-win' solutions is what we, as real estate entrepreneurs, should pride ourselves upon achieving.

Let the naysayers sit on the sidelines and talk about how we are taking advantage of poor, unsuspecting homeowners by "stealing" homes and making unconscionable profits. They will continue to judge us based upon a commonly held belief afforded to them by the unethical practices of a few. Meanwhile the vast majority of us will continue to be on the frontlines, crafting creative solutions to problems that the naysayers do not know and the government does not understand. Let's get one thing straight, we profit because the services we provide have value in the marketplace. What is great about us as real estate entrepreneurs is that while we profit, we are simultaneously helping our neighbors and assisting the American economy to 'get back on track.' I am not professing that we are supermen and women, but when the cape fits…

THE BASICS REMAIN UNCHANGED

No matter the economic climate, there are basic principles of real estate entrepreneurship that are constant. Successful real estate entrepreneurs concentrate on these principles, and avoid the things that 'suck up' our time without moving us closer to the ultimate goal of closing a deal. We can be assured we are taking steps toward success when we concentrate on the basic principles.

Finding sellers that need to sell is the engine that drives our business. Without motivated sellers, everything else is for naught. The means to accomplish this varies from direct mail, newspaper and online ads, bandit signs, magnetic vehicle signs, business cards, bird dogs, and countless other methods. Each of these attracts potential sellers either directly to us or to a second tier marketing medium such as our website. No matter the method of finding sellers, the fact remains that we must continually fill our pipeline full of leads, because our business is strictly a numbers game …no matter the economy.

In my experience, the next basic principle addresses the number one reason real estate entrepreneurs fail. That is, once sellers have contacted us, we must quickly sift through the leads 'separating the wheat from the chaff.' This principle is often referred to as prescreening. Time spent talking to homeowners that are unmotivated to sell is wasted, and can paralyze any real estate investment business. Similarly, continually calling unmotivated sellers and attempting to convince them that we are the answer to their problems only leads to frustration. We are not the answer for everyone and the sooner we realize that truth, the sooner we can begin leveraging our time and helping more of those who truly do need us.

The current economy has far too many sellers ready and willing to walk away from equity to spend time on those who have no intention of ever working with us. In truth, sellers never walk away from equity. They choose to trade equity for the value we bring to the deal - whether that value comes in the form of peace of mind or something else they desire. This prescreening process will always be paramount to any successful real estate entrepreneur. It is the number one difference between those that do and those that talk about doing. As our mentor Ron LeGrand often reminds us, we must "deal only with those people that want to deal with us and 'whack' the rest."

Once we have prescreened our leads and identified motivated sellers, the next basic principle is to construct and present offers. Negotiating skills never go out of vogue, but 'over-thinking' can be detrimental as well. The fact is that when we find a seller that needs to work with us we should be as clear and concise with our offer as we can be. The seller simply needs to understand how we can create the win-win solution everyone is seeking. Less is more in most cases. In those instances when we can sense that the homeowner wants to retain some semblance of control it is often beneficial to present multiple offers. Many times this means an 'all cash' offer and at least one offer based on terms.

The price associated with the 'all cash' offer is considerably less than other offers because no matter the economy – 'cash is king.' Offers based on terms can consist of taking over debt, often referred to as "subject to," split-funded offers, owner financing and numerous other buying strategies. By providing multiple offers to a seller, we give them an opportunity to retain some control in a situation where they may have previously felt powerless. In doing so we can create a solution to their economic problem and at the same time build rapport. No matter the state of the economy, when constructing and presenting offers, it is our creativity that largely determines the percentage of prescreened leads that we turn into successful deals.

Another basic principle that successful real estate entrepreneurs do not overlook is the power of a follow-up system. Very few real estate deals are struck during an initial contact. Proactive follow-up with those sellers that need to "simmer" is essential. All sellers' minds will change with time and circumstance, and an effective follow-up system capitalizes on this fact. Follow-up also ensures that required due diligence is completed. Due diligence includes items such as completing the necessary paperwork, checking title and scheduling the closing. No matter the economy, effective follow-up systems establish credibility and distinguish us from other investors.

The last basic principle that remains unchanged is the need to close quickly. Having our method of funding aligned with our eventual exit strategy is vital. For example, when we fund our purchase of a property with owner financing we often seek to sell with owner financing. This way we can create multiple pay days – cash up front, cash flow monthly and a backend profit when our new buyer cashes out of the property. *If buying right is where profit is created, then selling right is where profit is realized.*

ADAPTING STRATEGIES TO THE NEW ECONOMY

While the new economy has done nothing to change the basic principles of real estate entrepreneurship, it has affected the marketplace where those principles are practiced. Lean times in real estate have cleared out some of the speculators and many of those whose main strategy was to buy at retail price and rely on market appreciation to realize a profit. Warren Buffet said it best when he said, "Only when the tide goes out do you discover who's been swimming naked."

For those of us still clothed, we clearly see and are capitalizing on the opportunities that the new economy has dropped in our laps. Maybe we are in an area where real estate values continue to decline drastically. This is an opportunity for us to make deeply discounted offers and 'build in' hefty equity spreads. Maybe we are surrounded by neighborhoods where overleveraged homeowners are on the brink of losing their homes to foreclosure. This is an opportunity for us to profit through short sales or loan modifications. Maybe institutional lenders own much of the real estate in the area. This is an opportunity to profit through the purchase of bulk packages of bank owned property, otherwise known as REOs. Realistically, each of these situations likely exists in our area and the opportunities to profit are all around us.

To take advantage of these opportunities, real estate entrepreneurs must leverage their time and resources. Realtors can be tremendous assets that assist us in leveraging our time in the same way that private money lenders assist us in leveraging resources. Let's look at each of these separately.

Realtors that understand what we do are extremely valuable to us. They can search the MLS and bring us leads, submit our offers, and sometimes even negotiate our short sales. Those investors that see Realtors as competitors rather than partners are effectively eliminating a resource that can exponentially increase the number of deals that we close. By choosing the Realtors we work with wisely, we can leverage our time and also ensure them a steady flow of business, so that our relationship is mutually beneficial. Realtors looking to assure themselves consistent cash flow are happy to work with a real estate entrepreneur that buys and sells properties each month. Likewise, attempting to buy and sell multiple properties without having the benefit of the best Realtors to leverage our time is impractical in today's economy.

Like Realtors, private money lenders are essential to real estate entrepreneurs in the new economy. The rise in the number of foreclosures means that banks are currently sitting on billions of dollars worth of real estate. Fortunately, banks are not in the real estate business, they are in the business of lending money. These REO properties are nonperforming assets on their financial statements and literally restrict the amount of money they are allowed to lend. This creates a tremendous opportunity for us. Still, the only offers entertained by lending institutions are all cash offers. When we make offers with our own cash, there is a finite number of offers that we can make; however when leveraging the cash of private money lenders, the number of offers we can make is only limited by the amount of cash we are able to raise.

The new economy has made private lending very attractive for individuals looking to find a safe alternative to the stock market. What we offer to private money lenders is a predictable rate of return secured against real estate at a desirable loan-to-value ratio. What we gain from private money lenders is access to cash for acquiring, repairing and holding real estate at an interest rate far below that charged by a hard money lender. In very simple terms, private money lenders open the door to many opportunities, and real estate entrepreneurs looking to profit in the new economy should capitalize on yet another mutually beneficial relationship.

TIME TO STEP-UP TO THE PLATE

The incomparable Napoleon Hill wrote, "Opportunity often comes disguised in the form of misfortune, or temporary defeat."

Entrepreneurs who choose to be educated, bold, and creative will find that the new economy has ushered in opportunities for rapid wealth creation that we will likely never see again in our lifetime. It is no time to bury our heads in the sand and hope for the best. It is time to showcase our talents and generate massive profits in a marketplace that is begging for our knowledge and skills.

ABOUT NATHAN

Nathan became interested in creative real estate investment while completing a Masters Degree program at Tulane University. Guidance and mentorship from Ron LeGrand, Preston Ely and other leading real estate entrepreneurs has paved the way for Nathan to become an expert in creating win-win solutions to the most challenging real estate situations. He works with an impressive team of real estate professionals continually developing his business and helping distressed homeowners in his community and around the country. Nathan lives in Missouri where he enjoys the only thing more rewarding than his real estate entrepreneurship...his marriage to his wife Kelly. Contact Nathan by visiting www.HouseMustGo.com.

CHAPTER 13
THE GIFTS YOU NEVER KNEW YOU (ALREADY) HAD

by Philip Blackett

"What gifts does one need to break out of the corporate grind and become a successful entrepreneur in Ron's real estate world?"

After seeing numerous late-night infomercials, sitting on a number of webinars with real estate gurus, and observing what is on the other side of life for such successful real estate entrepreneurs, you are ready to leave – or at least temporarily vacate – the 'pasture' of corporate America to see what the world of real estate investing is really about.

Well, Dorothy, this is definitely not Kansas, for the prerequisites needed to hang around the water cooler and reside in 'cubicle-nation' may or may not suit you very well here. As you will see, I definitely learned the importance of these gifts during my short stint as a real estate investor. So, before you pack your boxes (and Toto), and make your trip down the 'green dollar road' of real estate, you should know of the seven gifts that you must possess inside before you can reside in Ron LeGrand's world for long - during your pursuit of financial freedom and happiness.

127

I. A SERVANT'S HEART

"Service to others is the rent you pay for your room here on earth" ~ *Muhammad Ali*

Every Sunday evening, I look forward to watching the next episode of ABC's Extreme Makeover: Home Edition, one of the best shows I have ever seen. This show sparked the inspiration inside me to pursue real estate investing unlike any other. If you are not familiar with what the show is, each week Ty Pennington and his crew travels around the country to find a deserving family or neighborhood who desperately needs their house(s) to be renovated or replaced. To this day, I have never ended an episode without wiping from my eyes the tears of joy - witnessing how the lives of so many families have been improved due to such good Samaritans helping out our fellow brothers and sisters in dire need of a fresh start. For so long, it has been my dream to be on one of those episodes to be able to have such a significant impact in someone's life for the better, despite whatever problems he/she may be facing.

What I realized shortly, after a few episodes, was that I did not have to be on this show in order to help out families who are in need of a 'clean slate' and a new beginning. As of this writing, Americans are struggling all over this nation from rising unemployment, depressed home values, and a rigid banking system. Foreclosure levels are sky-rocketing as families are pressed to find solutions on how to save their homes. With many mortgages upside-down and resetting to higher monthly payments, some people do not see any reason to continue paying them at the expense of other necessities such as food, education, and health care. Some people would much rather walk away and ruin their credit than to succumb to such 'financial torture.' In every neighborhood, there are distressed homeowners who need solutions to their property problems.

As the Millennial Real Estate Problem Solver, I see it to be my obligation to help as many families as possible take care of their real estate problems, whether it's helping them get rid of a property, stay in their homes or find a house that they can actually afford. What I love most about being a real estate investor is more about being a problem-solver to those in need. Whether someone is enduring bankruptcy, divorce, foreclosure, or the loss of a loved one, I want to do my part to help them move on with their lives, and not let their property be the reason why they cannot enjoy a happier and more fulfilling life.

Helping someone move on with a 'clean slate' without worry is more of a reward to me than any check that you can hand me…well almost. The point is that, to be a successful real estate investor, you have to look out for other people as well as yourself. Business will do well for you, the more people that you help with their problems. I run my business, believing that "the more people I help each day, the richer I feel on the inside and the wealthier I manifest on the outside."

There is an endless supply of people who need our help. Homeowners don't care how much you know until they know how much you care. Whether helping families or fellow investors, the person who opens his/her arms will be in business for a long time and will enjoy every minute of it, providing 'win-win' solutions to neighborhoods and communities all around.

II. YOUR PERSONAL "WHY"

"There is a defining moment in every person's life. Within that moment, everything that that person is, shines its brightest." ~ *Anonymous*

September 14, 2008 is a day that I will always remember. It was a dark Sunday evening and while most people were probably eating dinner with their families and enjoying quality time and pro football, I was slaving at my cubicle - poring over financial statements that had as much excitement to me 'as watching paint dry.' I was doing my very best to make a good impression, so I would have a good chance to receive a third-year promotion, but I felt conflicted in the process. Here I was, sacrificing my social life (and my health to some degree) working for a great company, but my heart was elsewhere and not in my work. I was no longer passionate about what I was doing. I remember when my manager first said that. At first, I immediately got nervous and started to defend myself, but then a calming aura of relief came over me and I resisted the temptation. He was right. However, it wasn't until this night that I truly believed it myself.

The night when it was announced that Lehman Brothers was filing bankruptcy confirmed my deep convictions of what I really wanted out of life. I saw the cameras stalk numerous "former" employees picking up their boxes and keepsakes with embarrassed looks, and feelings of shame and lower self-worth, as they now had to break the bad news to their families who depended on them to provide for their households. The realization of dedicated workers who put in over ten, twenty, or even thirty years of their lives with a company, but later get ushered out like dirty laundry or yesterday's trash, disturbed me deep inside. Their job security was breached. Their futures were now uncertain.

I realized that they were no different from me. Their firm was no different from mine or any other company. If a business goes through tough economic times, people's jobs are at stake. That's just the way the corporate world works, and that frightened me. Why were so many people buying into this, believing that this was what job security was really about? Are these the same people who are patiently awaiting their pensions and Social Security twenty years later? I didn't want to be a part of any situation where I wasn't in control of my destiny. I no longer felt comfortable leaving my future in the hands of another human being or company. If I was going to make it, I had to do it myself, and becoming a real estate entrepreneur was my route to true freedom.

That night, I went on Amazon and bought over 15 books on real estate and entrepreneurship, determined to find a way that better suited who I was, a career path more pleasing to my personality and purpose. I desired a life that was more pleasing, where "work-life balance" was not reserved for those near 60 in age, but also for those who desired it and knew how to maintain that balance, regardless of how young. I didn't know exactly where this trail would ultimately lead me, but I knew I could not be contained in my 'cage' anymore.

I believe that every entrepreneur, including those in real estate, has a defining moment that puts them at a crossroads where they have to choose which path to take, knowing that whatever decision they make will change their life forever. To be successful in real estate through good and bad times, it helps to have your own personal "Why" that propelled you to get started in the first place …a fervent desire that you no longer want to live life the way that you used to …a passionate cry from within to provide a better living for yourself and your loved ones, beyond what you have even dreamed of. That "Why" will remind you, even in your darkest moment where you feel tempted to go back to 'corporate cubicle-ville', that all this was not in vain, and to persist on the path until you reach your own promised land. Without a strong "Why," you will not survive long in the real estate world.

III. SUPPORT PARTNERS

"At times, our own light goes out and is rekindled by a spark from another person. Each of us has cause to think with deep gratitude of those who have lighted the flame within us." ~ *Albert Schweitzer*

My quarter-life crisis struck earlier than I thought. Coming off the phone, I had never been more unsure of myself or more frightened in my life. The person on the other line was my mother, who told me what she thought of my recent decision to steer clear of corporate America and to become a full-time real estate entrepreneur. In complete contrast to my bubbly excitement in giving her the news, she let me know that it was the "stupidest decision I could have ever made." Now, I was not completely naïve in thinking that she would 'welcome this epiphany with open arms', but I also did not anticipate the constant rumbling in my stomach after getting an earful of what she thought of me for 'making this jump.' I had to sit down just to keep myself in check, for the person who I depended on the most for encouragement and unconditional support vehemently opposed me following what the "books, videotapes, and seminars" pushed me to do.

Right before I started to second-guess and doubt the possibility of reaching financial freedom and personal fulfillment through real estate investing, I received a text message from one of my good friends Holly. I told her my situation with my mom, and she quickly revealed to me that this was part of my destiny that I was here to fulfill. After an hour of back-and-forth texting, I felt more at ease and ready to take that first step on my new path.

I can honestly say now that, if it was not for Holly answering my call, I would not be doing what I am doing now. I would have settled for another job at another firm, even if it did not suit me inside. On the journey down this yellow brick road, there will be many people that will come to you and question your motives in breaking away from the status quo. They will have many questions, and will keep asking until they can find a morsel of doubt within you, to feed ravenously on that doubt likelingering vultures. Ask me how I know this?

However, there are times that I remember when I left a Financial Services/Consulting career fair 15 minutes after I arrived, simply because I did not feel like I belonged there anymore. That help me regain focus and acceptance that I was meant to walk 'to the beat of my own drum.' ...No one else's drum! ... My drum! But as with all people, we cannot always be so self-reliant to make these life-changing decisions on our own. Sometimes, we need someone to remind us of what our true purpose/calling is, and not to settle until we found what it is we are here to do, and to do it with passion.

Every one of us has people that we admire, and hold their opinion in high regard, which can be both a good and bad thing. My mother only wants what is best for me. I believe that, but I also believe that I have to ultimately choose what is right for me. As she used to tell me, and I say this to you too, the only person who you ultimately have to hold accountable for the decisions you make in life is the man (woman) in the mirror. In retrospect, I realize that 'for an eagle to soar to new heights, it must first leave its nest.' Thank you Mom, for helping teach this eagle how to fly on its own! God bless the child that's got his own...that's got his own (remember that song?).

As I progress into my fledgling real estate investing career, I have a number of people serving as both positive and negative motivation for me to keep going. Some include family and friends who I have least expected. Others include complete strangers who I have met at Ron LeGrand's Quick Turn Real Estate School who have gradually become part of the core of my support group, even if they are twice as old as I am. The point is that no investor can truly make it alone, for one must have the support of someone, whether it is a spouse, best friend, college roommate, cubicle buddy, or even a mentor (or two).

IV. MENTORS

"Formal education will make you a living; self-education will make you a fortune." ~ *Jim Rohn*

I used to think it was cliché when every person I aspired to be like in corporate America told me that a huge component of his/her success was having a steady mentor in his/her life. I heard that all the time, so that it was becoming commonplace everywhere I went. Well, that also includes real estate. Unless you want to learn from the school of hard knocks and repeat the mistakes of so many, having at least one mentor will not only cut the learning curve by at least half, but also will equip you with the tools and confidence to handle whatever situation may come your way. In my short career in real estate investing, I quickly found out that I would not be anywhere close to where I am, or destined to be, if I did not have a few people in my life who have taught me not only the techniques to use, but also the 'millionaire mind-set' that I should have in order to better my chances of succeeding and achieving true freedom.

I have an issue with people who quickly talk about real estate investing as just a bunch of "books, tapes, and seminars" put together by opportunists 'trying to make a quick buck.' While I can understand where some of them are coming from, one has to understand that everything you learn comes from someone else who learned before you. The same type of education I learn on my own through 'home study' courses, books, online articles, live webinars, conference calls, and interactive seminars, is similar to any student learning from a textbook, teacher or test. In fact, these "mentors" of mine have taught me more than what can be regurgitated on any achievement test, for I have gained more self-respect, confidence, and belief in myself to be an entrepreneur than ever before. For your information, I am constantly reading books that deal with business, self-help, real estate, spiritual, and other matters. Reading is not only fundamental to your success, but it is also essential to your mental sanity and personal growth. In real estate, it is essential that you always continue to learn and master your craft, for strategies change over time as the economy moves through its cycles. Otherwise, you will quickly be left behind by your competition and/or use outdated methods that may get you nowhere but into trouble.

Mentors such as John MacNeil and Ron LeGrand have prepared me to become a transaction engineer, where I am versatile enough to know what to do when any potential deal comes my way, which is the best way to do real estate investing since it opens up more options for you. These economic times call for you to be flexible in how you handle leads that come to you, for the better you are at solving problems for more people in various situations, the more successful you ultimately will be. Mentors equip you to do all that is possible within your sphere of influence. Outside of that, you have to rely on something (someone) much greater to take care of the supernatural.

V. FAITH

"...With men, this is impossible, but with God, ALL things are possible." ~ Matthew 19:26

By now, I know what some of you readers are thinking: "Philip, you are ONLY twenty-five years old with the rest of your life ahead of you! Why in the world would you put it all at risk to be a real estate entrepreneur during the worst of times in a recession?" If you're not thinking that, I am surprised, for ever since I left Wall Street to pursue real estate full-time, I have been constantly bombarded with such questions and puzzled looks when I tell people what I am doing with my life at this stage. Yes, I had a great job working in New York City making six-figures straight out of college, more money than some people have ever made in their careers (and I'm not even counting bonuses or other perks). However, as with all things, there is a season for everything, and, after two years, my season was up following stocks and bonds. I decided to follow my heart and my growing passion to be my own boss and to control my own destiny, and not to leave it in the hands of another person or a corporation outside of my own.

What made me do all this? Faith. I believe that God has a greater purpose for me and wants me to go into a different direction than what was expected of me by my peers. I honestly did not know what was going to happen when I first arrived at Ron LeGrand's Quick Turn Real Estate School, but I knew that I belonged there and I would understand better in due time. Honestly, these past nine months have not been 'a crystal staircase' by any means while becoming an entrepreneur. After supporting myself until my savings account and 401K were depleted, I was living completely on faith - the same way when someone is driving on "E," yet his car is still moving despite the yellow light flashing on. There is only so much you can do while living on unemployment. My diet was obviously not the healthiest, living off of ramen noodles, pepperoni pizza, and water on most days. Each month, I had to choose which bills were top priorities to pay as I got my real estate business going, dividing up money between the light bill and direct mail marketing at times. It got to a point where I almost had a foreclosure on my own home. I remember the days where the temptation of going back to a regular job gnawed at me endlessly.

However, I knew that if I kept being persistent and faithful, things would improve. My faith was made stronger through much prayer and weekly sermons from Joel Osteen who helped me internalize that "It's My Time" now! I believe that I will be blessed with a breakthrough that will allow me to keep going and to build momentum in my business. When family members asked me if I had a plan B if plan A did not work, I would tell them succinctly that "there is no plan B, for plan A is going to work." It took some "brass balls" to say that at the risk of looking crazy to my relatives, but I had a strong burning desire inside of me that yearned for me to give it my all. I knew that if I kept trying to "play it safe" and diversify my efforts towards working on my business and preparing my resume that I would only do 'half-ass' work in real estate. I was willing to give it my all, for that was all I had. I had moved out of my family's hometown, graduated from college, and left Wall Street to live on my own in Jersey City. Coincidentally, this was also the time where I broke up with my girlfriend, so I really felt alone.

However, it was somewhat assuring to be on my own, for I knew that if I failed, it would just take me down. No one else. At 25, I could surely rebound off of this much quicker than if I was 45. For that reason, I better understand why it may be difficult for some older people to get into real estate full-time when they have growing families to support, multiple mortgages to pay, and a lifestyle that they are not willing to sacrifice temporarily for the opportunity of living life like no one else. I truly understand that I have made it this far not by my own strength, but by my growing faith that God will provide for all my needs as long as I gave it my very best in what I do.

Though these past few months were difficult for anyone to endure, I have grown stronger in the process and more sensitive to what fellow homeowners are feeling in this recession. Because of my close encounter with foreclosure, I can better relate to homeowners who are in pre-foreclosure or facing bankruptcy and the risk of losing it all. By being willing to suffer now, I feel more empowered to not only control my own destiny after being through the worst of it, but also help as many families as possible through their real estate problems, so they can move on with their lives on a clean slate.

You have to understand that, as with all things in life, everything will not always work the way we want them to. However, something I remind myself everyday in this business is that if I do my very best, God will indeed take care of the rest. There is only so much you can do on your own without driving yourself (or your spouse) crazy. There are only so many hours in the day to do what is necessary in your business. However, when you finally realize that you are not on this journey alone and that someone greater than you is watching out for you, it definitely makes the journey a lot smoother and enjoyable as a real estate entrepreneur.

VI. "BRASS BALLS"

"Freedom lies in being bold." ~ Robert Frost

One of my all-time favorite movies is *The Pursuit of Happiness* starring Will Smith, which features the story of Chris Gardner who arduously works his way from being homeless to working with a top-notch investment bank towards having his own firm. If there was one scene that made the movie, it was the basketball scene where Chris Gardner (Will Smith) told his son not to waste his time being a professional basketball player since Chris was below-average himself. His son was so disappointed and upset that he threw his basketball – and his aspirations – away. Chris later encouraged his son to go after his dreams and to never let anyone convince him otherwise.

That scene means so much to me, because I feel that everybody in life goes through something similar. Everyone has at least one dream that they always wanted to pursue. Oftentimes, we let other people's negativity, fear, or doubt cause us to second-guess whether or not our dreams are worth pursuing. When we succumb to that belief, we drift from reaching our full potential and settle for living a mediocre life. Anyone who chooses otherwise and strives to become much better than average, especially in real estate investing, has to have some "brass balls."

Now Ron LeGrand may have a different definition for "brass balls" than I do. I won't argue with him, since he arguably was the originator of the phrase. However, in my mind, "brass balls" can best be summed up as the willpower inside that refuses to settle for less in anything. A strong desire to be true to yourself and not a carbon copy of someone else. The necessary persistence to pursue your ambition as a real estate entrepreneur when everyone else thinks you are crazy. The unwillingness to give up and return to the corporate cubicle when a deal does not go your way. To me, "brass balls" means all these things because they keep you from quitting when you are so close to succeeding.

Tony Robbins mentioned that the reason why such people as Michael Jordan, Bill Gates, Oprah Winfrey, Muhammad Ali, and Mother Teresa are so great in our eyes is that these people refused to live an average life like everyone else. They had the "brass balls" inside to choose to raise their standards for themselves to the point of being "unreasonable." Whether it was their tireless work ethic, fervent passion for serving others, or burning desire to be the very best in their field, these people went the extra mile to achieve greatness no matter what obstacles came in their way.

As a real estate entrepreneur, I have never failed as many times here as in the rest of my life before. I grew up as the kid that succeeded in practically everything. I never took failure or disappointment well because I was not used to it. Becoming a real estate entrepreneur was enlightening to me, for what used to appear to me as mistakes and failures now became learning lessons and stepping stones. In order to get better, you cannot quit the moment things get rough or if you don't get your offer accepted. Persistence and follow-up are two of the most crucial elements towards success; for oftentimes, we move on to something else quickly if things don't work out the first time. Ron LeGrand reminds us that most of our business in real estate investing will come from the second to seventh contact you have with a potential seller. If you are one who is quickly dissuaded when you don't get called back as quickly after sending your first set of letters, you may be in for a lesson from the school of hard knocks.

I do not regret going the path less traveled by becoming a real estate entrepreneur full-time, for I understand that while it is probably rockier and less lit than the corporate path, I believe that the destination is much brighter than I can imagine. I believe that if I keep pushing through, things will eventually get easier and likely lead to a snowball / virtuous cycle in my business. The key to success is never to give up, and never be afraid to be bold in your own pursuit of happiness.

VII. A.T.O.M. (AGGRESSIVE TAKE OWNERSHIP MENTALITY)

"I'm trying to free your mind, Neo. But I can only show you the door. You're the one that has to walk through it."
~ *Morpheus (The Matrix)*

Over the past six months, I have been all over the country at numerous seminars and boot camps that taught me the many facets and strategies of real estate investing. Usually, I am one of the youngest people in attendance, as most people are in their mid-forties or early-fifties aiming to make the second half of their lives better than the first. For three to four days straight, hundreds of attendees will go over their booklets and miniature home study systems following along with the teacher. However, a realization irks me at the end of these boot camps, and Ron LeGrand knew way ahead of me what that frustration was.

No matter how much information that these attendees received, only a select few were actually going to implement these strategies when they got back home. I was introduced to the concept of "seminar junkies," people who quickly sign up with their wallets to go to every boot camp and seminar available. Yet for some reason, they are hesitant to do something significant about their situation when they get back home. Frankly, I don't understand it. If someone is taking you step-by-step on how to start-up your real estate business and how to set it on auto-pilot, why doesn't everyone do this as soon as they make it back home?

Out of all the "gifts" that I outline here, this may be the most crucial. An *aggressive, take ownership mentality* (A.T.O.M.) is absolutely essential for one to succeed as a real estate entrepreneur. As an atom is the building block of life, an A.T.O.M. is the very foundation that will determine if you will be successful or not. When you first get started, you cannot rely solely on others to set up your business for you, nor take a passive approach to finding leads. You have to be aggressive and capitalize on every opportunity that comes your way. If you do not, someone else will. If you operate a business, you have to take ownership so that it's yours and no one else's. Understand that no one will care as much about whether it survives, thrives, or fails, as you. You have to see yourself either as the lion or the gazelle in this jungle. No matter which one you see yourself as, you have to start each day running for your life or risk losing it. You can believe all you want that you don't have to put in your own sweat equity outside of positive thinking, but understand that faith without works is useless.

If you are a "thinker brain" as Ron likes to call them, this may take some effort over time, for while it doesn't hurt to analyze every possible scenario and outcome by mailing yellow letters yourself or hiring someone to do it for you, it doesn't necessarily help either. "Analysis paralysis" is a real debilitating epidemic among budding real estate entrepreneurs, for the time it takes you to make a firm decision could cost you multiple deals that could make you thousands and further delay you from living the life you always wanted to live. I can say this because I used to be a "thinker brain," until Ron converted me to a hybrid "thinker/reptile" brain who thinks quickly, acts quickly and then ponders about what to do next after the decision has already been made.

One of my mentors taught me that one of the things that separates the successful entrepreneur from your 'ho-hum' entrepreneur is the "speed of implementation." How long it takes you to transform an idea into action can make all the difference in your business, and also whether or not you are the trendsetter in your community or the 'dunce in the class.' The seminars and boot camps are best suited for the aggressive who are able to seize a concept and quickly implement it in their business within days of coming back home. Success comes quickly to those who simply make it happen now.

As Ron said, the only way to get better is to 'suck' first. You can't 'suck' until you try something for the first time and be persistent in getting better -until it becomes second nature. Oftentimes, we want to make sure that everything is perfect instead of getting it going first. You can always improve later. All in all, Ron LeGrand (and others) can show you the way to true freedom through real estate investing, but unless you are willing to take the initiative and consistently take action everyday towards achieving your goals, you may not be "The One" to become a successful real estate investor.

THE END OF THE ROAD

Now, for all those who remember the end of The Wizard of Oz, you will recall that Dorothy and her companions came to the Wizard looking for gifts to make their lives better. However, they all found out that each of them already possesses the gifts that they had always been looking for. They had to realize it for themselves once their moment of testing came. I bet you know where I'm going with this, huh?

Many times, we ask more of others than we ask of ourselves. I listed the seven gifts that I feel are necessary for anyone to be an extremely successful real estate investor. However, you must realize that these gifts cannot be given to you by someone else, not even by the Wizard (Ron). These are gifts that you must have internally or cultivate during your journey. The good news is that while the journey is not necessarily a 'walk in the park', if you use these seven gifts to the best of your ability, you'll be amazed at the kind of person you will evolve into – as well as the extraordinary life that you create – at the end of the road. When you become a successful real estate investor, trust me…there's no place like it!

ABOUT PHILIP

After graduating from the University of North Carolina at Chapel Hill, Philip Blackett worked for two years as an Equity Research Analyst at Goldman, Sachs & Co. in New York City. He then decided to "retire" from Corporate America and become a real estate entrepreneur full-time, and he is now the President of Win/Win Redevelopment Corporation and the owner of Clean Slate Properties, LLC.

As a budding social entrepreneur, he has dedicated his life to providing affordable housing, redeveloping communities nationwide, and solving the problems of distressed homeowners with 'win-win' solutions. As a real estate investor, Philip has focused his attention on fulfilling his mission to help at least 10,000 distressed homeowners nationwide save their houses from foreclosure through the use of forensic audits.

For more information on Philip, please visit his blog websites at: www.PhilipBlackett.com and: www.MisterPotential.com, as well as his real estate websites at: www.SaveMyHouses.com and: www.plssellmyhouse.com. He is also on Facebook, LinkedIn, and Twitter (@PhilipBlackett).

CHAPTER 14
MARKETING HOUSES AT NO RISK

by Brian Snyder

I t all started in 2004. I started in this business buying rental proper-ties. I bought a duplex so I could live in one side and rent the other side. This way I could offset most of my mortgage payment. I quick-ly found out that this was not as easy as it seemed, as I had tenants that I had to evict and clean up after - within the first year of owning my duplex. I knew there had to be a better way to be successful in real es-tate than going to court hearings to gain possession of my property and throwing out the junk left behind by deadbeat tenants. Furthermore, after buying, fixing, and refinancing my second property I also found out that the banks wanted a ridiculous amount of money down to give me loans for properties that I did not live in. Then, even if I wanted to put at least 20% down, I could not buy many more properties with bank financing, as they decided that I did not make enough money to qualify for many more loans.

At that time I talked to a couple of people that I knew had some proper-ties, and they referred me to a weekend seminar which was coming up in a few weeks at our local R.E.I.A. Club (R.E.I.A. stands for Real Estate Investors Association which is a local networking group of investors). These groups are all over the country in a city near you. I highly recommend you join this group, the annual fee is cheap compared to the people you will meet and the information you will learn. So I went to this three day event at my local club. I listened to about twenty different speakers talk about taxes, apartment buildings, rehabbing distressed properties, taking over debt, and wholesaling. I wanted to invest in every course that was being offered for sale, but I could not afford to do that, so I listened to all the speakers, and decided the one for me was being offered by a speaker named Ron LeGrand. I bought Ron's materials and began listening to the CD's and reading the material. I also attended Ron's event several months later dealing with "ugly" houses, and how to profit from them. I learned this could be done without ever owning them or fixing one single thing! In fact the uglier the house, the better the deal! This workshop changed my outlook on the real estate business, and how I approached it... no more tenants and bank mortgages for me!

The topic that I was most attracted to was a concept known as wholesaling. Wholesaling can be summarized simply as finding bargain properties and passing them onto buyers looking for bargain deals and getting paid to do so. You never have to buy the property, you never have to fix the property, *and most importantly you do not have to have money or take* any *risk to do these deals!*

Here is how it works. You find a motivated seller that is willing to sell their property at a price that would be attractive to an investor to buy for all cash. You get that property under contract with the seller. Then you market this property at a higher price to investors. Please note that you should not get greedy. You want to make at least several thousand dollars, but leave the "meat on the bone" for the end-buyer to profit from the property. Once you identify your buyer, you want to assign them your contract (this is how you get paid). This is known as an *assignment of contract*. This is your fee (profit) for finding the deal and passing it along to a buyer. You never own the house, you never fix the house, and you have no monetary risk in the house.

You want to find the ugliest houses in neighborhoods where investors want to buy. My favorite story of a deal I have done came in June of 2006. I was driving with my realtor looking at some properties for sale. On our drive home there was an accident and we had to take a detour. We drove down the detour and saw a 'run down' looking house for sale. We stopped to look at it. It was a foreclosure. It was overpriced, and needed a lot of work. This was not a deal, but the deal was the house next door. The property next door was a duplex that had severe fire damage. The owner was sitting on the front porch and we got to talking. He said the house had burned about 7 months prior and the city wanted it fixed or torn down, and he had to make a decision within a month or the city would step in and tear it down out of safety concerns. He said that he and his wife had another house they were living in, and did not want to spend the $16,000 needed to tear it down, and certainly did not want to deal with fixing it. He was asking $15,000 for the property. I looked in the front door and said I was not interested in seeing it as it was unsafe to walk through. I offered him $2,000 for it. He said no. However, I continued to explain that if he took a minute to think about it, I was actually offering $18,000 ($2,000 in cash to buy it and $16,000 he would be saving by not having to tear it down). After I presented it that way, he agreed. I had a house under agreement for $2,000, but I certainly did not want to deal with the renovation. I decided to whole-sale it. I went to Office Max and bought a bright pink poster board and a fat Sharpie marker and wrote the following on it…

> For Sale
> Handyman Special
> Cheap/Cash
> 412-XXX-XXXX" *(I obviously put my phone number in place if the X's)*"

Now my handwriting is about equal to that of your average 5th grader, so this sign was ugly. Add to it the fact that it was duct (not duck) taped to the front window on an angle, and on a very heavily fire-damaged house this was about the ugliest sign you have ever seen. It was so ugly that I received about five calls within two hours of putting the sign up, and I sold that house for $5,500 in two days. I will not say my risk was zero on this house, as I did give the seller a $10 deposit, I spent $27.88 on marketing materials (Sharpie marker, poster board, and I also had to buy a padlock to secure the property as the owner had the doors nailed shut). I had $37.88 out of pocket on this deal, and got several thousand dollars in return on that deal. It was a win/win/win/win deal. The seller won as he sold the property, and did not have to tear it down costing him thousands. The buyer won as he got a cheap duplex that he fixed and resold to a landlord and made money. I won as I made a 'couple thousand' on the wholesale. Finally, the city and neighborhood won as they got an eyesore fixed and back on the tax rolls!

The most common question that is asked is "where do I find these deals." The answer is they are all around - you just have to be looking for them. I know the burned duplex is an obvious one, but there are thousands of less obvious houses out there that are great prospects. If snow falls where you live, look for houses that do not have the snow shoveled in the winter. In the spring, summer, and fall, look for houses that do not have the grass cut or the leaves raked. Look for mail or newspapers piling up. Your local city government may be able to help. You can contact your local code enforcement officer. They may be willing to share with you addresses of properties that are condemned or being fined. There are few things that will motivate a seller more than having the city condemn a property. Also, do not think a house has to be ready to fall down to be condemned, I know of properties that have been condemned due to the simple fact that a front window was broken and the owner never fixed it. A new $300 window and the house was off the condemned list! Other ways to find motivated sellers could be as simple as calling F.S.B.O. (For Sale by Owner) and For Rent ads in the newspaper. There are thousands of people around the country at any given time that have a house they need to sell, but they think they cannot because it needs work or is in a bad area. They then try to sell 'by owner' instead of with a realtor or rent it and become landlords. Many of these people would love to sell if a cash offer came along. You can provide the cash offer they are looking for!

You might be saying "I do not have time to do these things." Well, I suggest you hire what Ron calls an "Ant Farm." Hire people to drive neighborhoods, call ads in the paper, talk to city code enforcement, etc., and bring the leads back to you. You can pay them per lead or per deal you complete. This is a great way to get more leads than you know what to do with, and deals will come from those leads!

I have a deal, now what? The first thing you need to do once you have a deal is get an agreement signed with the seller. This is done through an *Option to Purchase*. In this chapter I cannot supply you with one, so I suggest you visit my website at: www.MarketingHousesAtNoRisk. com to gain access to all the forms I use everyday. You can also contact a local closing attorney so that they can supply you with one that is acceptable. Please note that it may take a few phone calls to find an attorney who completely understands what you are looking to do. Do not get discouraged if this happens, just know it is legal everywhere, and you may have to go through a few people to find the one you are looking for. The option agreement allows you to tie up the property but does not obligate you to buy it. You have the right to market the deal and assign your rights to it for a fee using an assignment of contract form. Again, see your attorney for this form. When your end buyer signs the assignment of contract, get a deposit check and send all of the paperwork to the closing attorney you are working with. They will then do the customary closing process, and when closing occurs, the attorney will send you a check for the balance of the assignment fee you are due. Note that you are not the buyer or the seller, therefore you are not paying closing costs. You get 100% of the assignment fee.

I mentioned my ugly pink sign in the window of the 'burned out' house before, but there are many more ways to market properties other than a sign. I highly recommend you put a sign out in front of the house you are selling, however I have 2 tips:-

#1: Make sure you get the sellers permission to do so. Remember, often times these houses are vacant and the seller may not want everybody who drives past to know it is for sale.

#2: The sign should be ugly. Hand written is best. The more you stand out from all the nice realtor signs the better! You can get sign shops to make you signs that look hand written.

Please visit: www.mybanditsigns.com to buy signs direct from the same place I get my signs from. I suggest getting yellow signs with black letters. Be sure to get the letters in a font that looks like hand writing (in other words it looks homemade). There are many other free ways to market your properties. I use Craigslist for every property I am selling. I create a free flier at: www.postlets.com and then post this flier on Craigslist. Do not post just one time. I have my properties re-posted every Monday and Friday. I get many calls from people looking on Craigslist. You may also run an ad in the classified section of your local paper or craigslist. The ad below was created by Ron, and it works! It should read exactly like this:-

Handyman Special
Cheap/ Cash
Your phone Number
(Please remember to substitute "Your Phone Number" with your actual phone number... if you don't, I promise your phone will not ring!)

That's it! That's the magic ad! I would also have a blank line above and below it, so your ad will actually be 5 lines with only 3 lines of text. You can make the text bold if you wish. Your local paper may require you to write 'handyperson' or something other than handyman but run 'handyman special' if you can, keep it simple! Remember to record the name, number, e-mail address of everybody that calls you. Start to build your buyers list. Once you start to build your list, you can email this list of all the new properties you get. Be sure to advertise your houses for sale at your local R.E.I.A. groups as well. Before you know it, you will have many buyers on your list and all you will have to do is e-mail them properties, and they will buy them. Just remember; always grow your list with the techniques above. There are always buyers out there looking for deals, you want as many of them as possible looking to you for them!

There are thousands of people buying investment properties today. Most of them are fighting over realtor listings and likely paying too much for these deals. I want you to become a trusted provider of investment properties to your buyers in your city. There are deals out there nobody knows about. I have given you a few tips on how to go find them, and sell them to the investors in your database and make thousands of dollars per transaction. It is a great way to create monthly cash flow, and best of all: <u>you do not need to risk any money to get deals done.</u> The market does not matter, your credit does not matter, and your bank account balance does not matter. All you need is determination and some time in order to get your 'marketing-houses-at-no-risk' system started. From there, the sky is the limit!

ABOUT BRIAN

Brian Snyder lives in Pittsburgh, PA, and has been buying and selling houses since 2004. In that time he has done a wide range of deals including wholesale, rehabs, short sales, owner financing, and subject-to. He has sold properties in various ways as well including wholesaling to a cash buyer, selling retail to owner-occupants through realtors and by owner, owner financing, and the rent-to-own program.

Brian attributes his success to the help of others. In 2006 Brian joined a mentoring program in Pittsburgh. Learning from other experienced investors dramatically improved his learning curve. As a result, in 2008, he decided to give back to others as well. Brian began working with his mentors and helped to expand their program to include many more students in Western Pennsylvania. The group now includes students throughout the United States. These students are currently closing profitable real estate transactions in different markets throughout the country. Brian is also proud to work for Ron LeGrand as a mentor in his mentoring program - which currently has students in the United States and Canada.

As you know by reading the chapter titled Marketing Houses at No Risk, Brian's favorite way to profit in real estate is to wholesale properties. Therefore he has launched an educational website that teaches wholesaling step-by-step. Everything you need to know to get started is there, as well as information to take you to the next level. To gain access to this valuable information and get a free report titled "The #1 mistake many real estate investors make when starting their wholesale business" for free; visit: www.MarketingHousesAtNoRisk.com. You will see all of the tools that he uses everyday in his business. This is the best deal you will find to get information about the topic of wholesaling houses, and he knows you will find it extremely resourceful, educational, and helpful.

www.MarketingHousesAtNoRisk.com

CHAPTER 15
YOUR PERSONAL GUIDE TO FREEDOM

REASONS TO SETUP & AUTOMATE YOUR REAL ESTATE BUSINESS

by Christine Brown, CPA

So you've decided to be free, to follow your own dreams, make your own way, be your own boss and start your own business. Your industry of choice is Real Estate - CONGRATULATIONS!

Let's get real for a moment. Maybe the truth is more like this wonderful market has decided to FREE you! Maybe it freed you from your job, freed you from your hard earned savings, freed you from your 'once stellar' credit rating, and perhaps even freed you from your home. And now without the demanding weight of trying to juggle all of those balls (*because they have all hit the ground with a resounding thud*), you have nothing… and I do mean NOTHING but time!

TIME is that once rare commodity that less than two years ago you would have sold a kidney to have more. You figured, "ah why not,

I only need one to live anyway." Hell, if you are one of the few and fortunate that didn't receive your freedom in the form of a "pink slip" accompanied by an all expense paid trip…to the unemployment office, you still just might be willing to sell that kidney for some more TIME. That is if you only had the TIME to search the web or place an ad on Craig's list to find a buyer.

Can you believe this mess? You are now either doing the job of three people for the luxury of not joining the unemployment line and/or the homeless (*raise?…bonus?… what are those?);* or you are going crazy with nothing but time to play over and over again how your life has not turned out as you imagined it would. Maybe you are trying to figure out where it all went so wrong? Like so many people, perhaps you are thinking, "How did the American Dream turn into a nightmare? Why didn't we see it coming and who's to blame? Somebody should be shot, horse whipped, and their body hung up in the street as a warning to anyone else who dares to try and screw us again. Is this supposed to be the wonderful future we all dreamed of and worked so hard to get to?"

With all the advances made by "man" both technological and morally, [lighting fast technology that allows you to push a button on your computer one minute and be face-to-face with a person on the other side of the world; advancements within medical science that has figured out how to clone life, a sacred duty once reserved only for God; and with the election of a black man to the Presidency of the United States, a country literally built on the backs of his ancestors] you would think in the twenty-first century we would have figured out by now how to have both TIME and MONEY. But no, those with money have no time, and those with time have no money!

That's the real rub, isn't? A few years ago when we were all fat, happy, and comfortable (*although most of us didn't realize it*), we had plenty of money or at least credit. Remember the days when laws had to be written to stop companies from sending "live" unsolicited credit cards out in the mail? Well let's not go there; that's another book. Back then we had money but no time to enjoy it. I can remember having to plan a one week vacation at least six months in advance; two weeks was simply out of the question. I still don't understand how other countries have managed for centuries to allow their employees to take a four-week holiday annually, while the only way America has managed to grant that much time-off is with this great 'depression'...oops! ...I mean recession!

Well, regardless of whichever of life's forces that have shaped your path, pursuing freedom by choice or if you are trying to avoid being killed by the overdose of time with no money heaped on your head, it has brought you here... to this moment... to this book... and to me.

So let us use this gift of time wisely and do our best to discover the answer to gaining true freedom. Freedom simply means having available time and the money needed to enjoy it. I call it "Freedom to Purpose," financial freedom allows us time to pursue our life's purpose...the purpose for which we were born, the reason we were created.

Surely our purpose on this earth was meant to be more than just putting in 10 to 13 hour days (including commuting and overtime); some of us work ourselves into obesity, depression, and/or an early grave - just for the privilege of living in a house a lot of us will never actually own, driving 'earth polluting' cars that are sometimes beyond our budget, and/or eating (*all to often*) the so called "food" that has had all of the nutrition processed or cooked out of it. It seems like we are in debt almost from birth, convinced by mass media that we just have to have the next great "widget" in order to be happy, accepted, or find love. Is it any wonder why our culture is in the shape it's in today when sex is used to sell everything, even a mop for heaven sake ('*love hurts ya, ya,*' ...the commercial sings)!

Okay...I know that by now a lot of you are scratching your head and glancing back to the "written by" line thinking, "didn't it say this writer is a CPA; that does stand for Certified Public Accountant doesn't it? Surely this 'mad' woman is kidding; she doesn't expect me to buy that, does she? 'Number crunchers' just don't have that much personality"! Well, YES, yes I do and yes I am. As entertaining as this chapter may have been so far, you know it was coming. It is time to get down to business. This is a book on Real Estate and a chapter on reasons to setup and automate your business, after all.

Let's begin with a brief introduction before you started on your road to FREEDOM. I am a CPA with more than 20 years of experience in Accounting, Audit, Operations, Compliance and Operational Risk

Management. I have worked in the Not-For-Profit, Public Accounting and Financial Service Industries; from credit unions to a Fortune 100 company. I have had the unique fortune of walking into company after company just in time to have the already huge mess that I was hired to clean up explode as soon as I accepted the position and cleared the doorway. My professional claim to fame has been, "if it's broke I can fix it, or at least give you some great ideas on how it should be fixed" - that's what Auditors do.

Now, after my forced freedom from an often stressful stint in Corporate America, where I was dutifully working at my 'officer level' position at a bank, blissfully unaware that my industry was about to be the 'ground zero' of the perfect financial storm that would shake America to its very knees, I have embarked on my own personal journey to freedom. Like you, I saw Real Estate as a potential means to gain true freedom: both time and money. But a funny thing happened to me while I was making my way into the wonderful world of Real Estate; I kept running into these innovative, positive, never-say-die entrepreneurs. I met a lot of them as fellow students in Ron LeGrand's Master Real Estate Entrepreneur program. After talking to several of them, hearing their stories of long hard hours, triumphs and failures, and listening to Ron tell us about many of his students' failure to take the required actions to succeed; a pattern started to emerge.

Though armed with the vast knowledge that Ron provides in his classes, often these innovative, energetic entrepreneurs seemed to be enslaved by the very businesses that they created to free themselves. If they are not careful they could wake up 10, 20 or 30 years from now to find that they have missed their children growing up, they no longer know the love of their life, and they never got to explore their life's purpose. Why? Maybe because they have served a hard task master that replaced one job with 10 and turned an 8 hour workday into 16 hours; for better pay, yes, as long as they never took a vacation and kept up an impossible pace.

Entrepreneurs often provide a great life for those around them, but for many at the cost of their own. This is largely due to their inability to adapt from a *creation business model*, where they do everything themselves, to a *growth model* that develops adequate organization and automation. They end up too 'caught up' in the details and the false glory of being the only one who can "get it done," to realize that the price of their success is the very freedom they desired in the first place. This vicious cycle must and can be stopped.

It is to this end that I created Freedom Consulting and Training, a service aimed at teaching entrepreneurs how to view their business from an aerial approach ("top-down") to ensure success and freedom, instead of being wrapped up in the day-to-day details of business. Based on my 20 years of experience "fixing" businesses, I have created this simple model to provide entrepreneurs with a better understanding of what it takes to run a business, from startups to experienced owners. I believe that all businesses, small or large, are comprised of these basic business components:

STRATEGY & PLANNING			
LEGAL & COMPLIANCE	**MARKETING**	**OPERATIONS**	**ACCOUNTING & TAXES**
INFORMATION & TECHNOLOGY			

Let us discuss each component briefly:

Strategy and Planning - The business plan &/or model developed to govern the business; the mission, goals & objectives, strategies, management, policies, and processes by which the business is operated; the type of products or services offered; phases of growth expected; methods of funding the business; and budget projections used to ensure profitability (which compares projected income and expenses for resources needed - both human & others).

Legal & Compliance – The process used to ensure that all governing agencies, required laws, and regulations are known by a business for that business' industry, and consistent compliance is maintained.

Marketing – The plan that defines the business' target market, sets pricing, develops a competitive edge, determines strategies & methods used to reach that market and converts them into customers. The marketing plan should support the expected growth phases and budget projections.

Operations – The day-to-day processes used to ensure that quality products or services are provided to customers efficiently, consistently, and timely (revenue producer); and that the business is secured, properly staffed, and has adequate resources to maintain function (administrative).

Accounting & Taxes – The process used to ensure that all assets, liabilities, equity and transactions are properly recorded to compile the business' financial data into information (Financial Statements and other reports) required to make management decisions, secure financing, and comply with IRS tax laws. To be effective, financial records must be complete and properly classified, with entries recorded in the correct accounting period.

Information & Technology – The ongoing process used to ensure that relevant information (strategies, policies, procedures, and business data, i.e., sales, financial data, customer feedback, market changes, special instructions, etc.), flows consistently and efficiently throughout the business. Technology is the system used to house, carry, and store such information.

As this model clearly demonstrates, Strategy & Planning must be the first component completed to create the business plan, because if it is done thoroughly, it is the foundation that will support the business - allowing it to grow. However, like Information & Technology (IT), it is an ongoing component that must be considered at every stage of business. While IT is the method for carrying out the business plan; the other four components discussed should be performed sequentially, and detail "how" the plan will be implemented.

All of these components and related processes must be done to allow your business to grow, become self sustaining, and support your quest for freedom. However, it is just as imperative that you understand that you **CAN NOT** and **MUST NOT** be the person performing all of them! There is **NO** freedom in that. This is where the wonderful art of delegation and the science of automation come in.

Whether you are just starting your business or have been operational for a while, take a minute to think about each of these components and ask yourself if they exist in your plan or business? What I have seen time and time again is that often excited, energetic entrepreneurs jump 'head first' into "Operations" - quickly figuring out that they must do some form of "Accounting" to eventually pay "Taxes," so they purchase "Technology," usually QuickBooks. But the other components are often missing or lacking.

Depending on the business, necessary attention is paid to the supplies and facilities; entrepreneurs do whatever it takes to make the sale. "HOORAY, it worked, I told them it would," they proclaim! Now they can prove to all of the lovely 'vision killers' in their life, whose responses ranged from "You're going into business for yourself? Ooh, ...I wouldn't do that if I were you" to "Are you f---ing nuts? In this economy you had better get two or three part-time jobs like everyone else. I think McDonalds is hiring," ...proving that they aren't crazy after all.

There is only one little problem, the expense train is still moving. Now they must support both home and the business. The victory of their first win is short lived as 'never ending' bills bring them back to earth quickly! Then the realization suddenly hits them that everything that they did to get that first sale (*all of the fear they faced, all of the hard work, all the worry and sleepless nights, even the plain dumb luck*), must be immediately repeated in order for them to stay in business and they have already 'tapped out' all of their family and friends. So being the 'never say die', 'face against the wind' people that they are, these fearless entrepreneurs stick their chest out, hold their heads up, and get to work to "get it done"...giving up any hope for their desire for freedom that started this madness in the first place.

It is no wonder why 40% of new businesses fail in year 1 and 80% by year 5. No matter how intelligent, determined, or 'downright stubborn' a person is, no one can run on a never-ending treadmill forever. Repeat after me: "I must create standardized policies & processes, hire & train people to do those processes, and/or purchase technology to automate every part of my business that is possible!"

I know some of you are like me (*went to school on the short bus*); a bit S-L-O-W. So I will say it another way; if you are the only one who can do it right, you will be the only one doing it...FOREVER! So when your family heads off for a luxury vacation that your new found wealth affords, or does its duty to help boost this sagging economy by going shopping on the avenue, or chooses that new luxury car that you have been wanting so badly and you just can't get away from "the business" (your new boss) long enough to join them, remember you have been warned. Get it!

Now, I know some of you are going to take this warning too far. So for those of you who have now gone from, "I can do it all myself. I trust no one with my business" to "Hell, if I will miss out on all of that fun which I'm paying for, I will hire 10 people tomorrow and let them do all of the work"; (*you know who you are*), let me put it into perspective for you. What you absolutely **MUST** do yourself is drive revenue (which means making sure that customers are showing up to buy your widgets); ensure that adequate controls and reporting exist to provide you with confidence that your business is running as designed; ensure that customers are getting quality products or services; ensure that taxes are recorded and paid; and that no one is running off with your profits ...for that matter, *that there are profits!*

I know, that sounds a lot like work, doesn't it? It is. No one said FREE-DOM was free! But note what I **DIDN'T SAY**: I didn't say create the product or perform the service yourself, develop the marketing, run the campaign, build the website, design & clean the office, serve the customers, handle all the money, pay all of the bills, do the accounting, and get Turbo Tax to file the return yourself. Does this sound like someone you know? (...*You know who you are, so I won't call any names.*)

NO, it's your job as owner to create the plan that outlines the business strategy and ensure that adequate policies, procedures, and monitoring reports governing all 6 business components exist, as well as maintaining facility, technology, and trained people (hire or contracted) to get it all done.

I am sure that some of you may have a lot of detailed questions on how to do your job as owner; but hey, I only have one chapter to work with here. Remember the idea was to get you started on your road to FREE-DOM, I never promised to get you there. Well, at least not in this single chapter of Ron's book; even I, "Ms. Fix It," can't pull that off.

This concludes the lesson I have been sharing with you: know your limitations, prioritize your time, efforts, and resources. Focus on doing the things in your business that no one else can or will do for you to make you FREE; automate, delegate, and monitor the rest! Not to worry if you want more information, advice, training or just want someone to do it for you *(again you know who you are and it is probably some of the same ones as before);* visit my website at www.FreedomConsulting.biz or e-mail me at freedom2purpose@yahoo.com.

Now that we are such great friends, please feel free to contact me and let me know how things are going. Good luck on your journey to FREEDOM… 'kick butt', 'take names', and most importantly…**have fun and enjoy the trip!**

ABOUT CHRISTINE

Christine Brown is a Certified Public Accountant (CPA), with more than 20 years of experience in Accounting, Audit, Operations, Compliance and Operational Risk Management. She has worked in the Not-For-Profit, Public Accounting and Financial Service Industries; from credit unions to a fortune 100 company. Widely known as "MS FIX IT," Christine has had the unique fortune of walking into company after company just in time to have the already huge mess that she was hired to clean up explode as soon as she accepted the position and cleared the doorway. Most of her career has required her to create and develop complex business solutions under critical deadlines, on a shoestring budget, from a blank sheet of paper.

Christine's fun loving, warm hearted, and creative hands-on approach to working with people combined with her excellent and uncompromising commend of business processes and the internal controls required for their success; makes her an awesome champion of change. She believes that "Life" is meant to be lived "Out Loud" filled with joy, passion, and above all FREEDOM!!!

It is this passion that drove Christine to start Freedom Consulting and Training LLC, dedicated to freeing entrepreneurs and business professionals from the deadly clutches of "Doing Business Badly." Too often innovative, energetic entrepreneurs become enslaved by the very businesses that they have created to free themselves; and business professionals watch year after year as their jobs consume more and more of their lives and reward them less and less. Freedom can only be gained by systemizing and automating processes to allow them to become self sustaining, thus freeing "you." To learn more about Christine Brown and how **you** can get your **FREE** business or training consultation visit her website www.FreedomConsulting.biz, e-mail her at freedom2purpose@yahoo.com or call her at 773-878-2259. She would love to serve you and help get you onto your own "Road to FREEDOM"!

CHAPTER 16
GOBS OF TAX-FREE MONEY AVAILABLE FOR REAL ESTATE INVESTING

by Rick Donner, CPA

You may be asking yourself if there is any good news on the economy. Most media outlets are constantly talking about the negative effects of the economic downturn. They neglect to mention that a recessionary economy presents a multitude of opportunities for those "in the know" to realize significant returns on their investments. How do I know this? For one, I'm currently experiencing great returns on my own investment activities. Second, the 1930's depression created more millionaires than at any time in history. And history repeats itself.

Stocks and other traditional financial instruments are not providing the kind of returns that are going to provide us with a comfortable retirement. In fact, many of us have lost a significant amount of the value of our portfolios due to our investment in these 'vehicles.' As 2006 Nobel Prize winner in economics, Edmund Phelps observed: "it may take up to 15 years for families to recover the wealth lost due to the recession." I'm not going to dispute a Nobel Prize winner; however, I am going to show you a way to significantly reduce that time frame and get your investment portfolio back in the winner's circle.

SOME ALARMING STATISTICS ON RETIREMENT

I don't want to go too deep into the health of our country's Social Security system except to say that if you are counting on it to provide for you in your retirement years, you may want to rethink that strategy. The Employee Benefits Research Institute reports that 26% of current retirees are just getting by each month. In a 1996 survey, they found that only 3% of current workers are very confident that Social Security will be available to them at today's benefit levels. It doesn't actually give you a secure feeling, does it? Let's have a quick look at some other alarming statistics:

- Approximately 1 in 10 Americans will reach financial stability upon retirement
- Only 5% of retirees have adequate capital to maintain their lifestyle throughout their retirement
- Approximately 3% of workers aged 65 or older have to continue working – mostly in lower paid jobs.
- An astounding 63% are dependent on Social Security
- A number of retirees report that their standard of living has significantly declined as compared to their working years
- It is estimated that a couple retiring today would need $215,000 for health care costs over a 20-year period.

These are truly frightening statistics for a nation as wealthy as ours. But enough of the bad news. I'm writing to you in an effort to keep you from being one of these statistics. Imagine gaining control of your own investment portfolio, producing investment returns that actually increase your portfolio's value, and diversifying your holdings to achieve better results. It's the same system that my wife Lisa and I use to produce exceptional results.

WHO AM I AND WHY SHOULD YOU LISTEN TO ME?

My name is Rick Donner and I am a practicing CPA in Fort Myers, Florida. I prepare a lot of tax returns for clients; however, I've become more choosy in the clients I take on. I have the discretion to do that due to the investment income my wife Lisa and I generate from our real estate holdings. Lisa and I met at a church in 1999 and were married three years later. We discovered that we both had a passion for real estate investing. One day we received a postcard to attend a free real estate investing seminar and our journey began.

We've attended many real estate investing seminars and classes over the years; however, this first seminar stands out in our memories. You see, we made our first deal within 60 days of that seminar that netted us $120,000. We were hooked and have done many deals over the years. Lisa and I have worked with a variety of private investors since then and have allowed them to share in our success. We specialize in producing win-win results **and teach others to do the same.**

I'm not sure if there has ever been a better time for capitalizing on the real estate market. Residential real estate is available at bargain rates for those with available cash reserves. Now if you're saying to yourself "I don't have extra cash for investing in real estate," allow me to explain to you how you can get your hands on 'gobs' of tax-free money if you know where to look.

Most investment advisors won't divulge this source of funds because they don't earn any fees from it. They want you to keep your investments in stocks, bonds, and CD's where they can take their cut of the proceeds. I'm talking about self-directed retirement plans where you can create diversity in your retirement portfolio and earn tax-free returns at the same time. As one of our clients observed:

"I had the opportunity to help Rick Donner with some investment opportunities. I was looking for a good return on retirement funds. I was able to loan Rick money for private mortgages. This has been one of my **best** decisions in years! <u>I receive a hefty return on my money with no rental hassles</u>. I receive consistent income with absolutely no problems. Rick & Lisa pay on time or sooner every month and I feel secure as the mortgagee on the title and the insurance policy. This has been one of **the** best win/win situations I have ever seen! Rick & Lisa are true professionals and I would recommend their partnership with anyone." - Mike P., Cape Coral, FL

THE BENEFITS TO DIVERSIFYING SELF-DIRECTED RETIREMENT PLANS

We've all heard about the benefits of portfolio diversification. It allows us to spread our investments over a wide range of vehicles in order to provide stability to our holdings. We are able to accomplish this by moving our investments into self-directed retirement plans including ROTH, SEP, 401K, and Education IRA's. In fact, most retirement plans can be used. Here, I will call it a real estate IRA to keep it simple. Just remember – this is a well kept secret – that is why you probably have not heard about real estate IRA's from your broker or banker. When we do this we allow ourselves to invest in traditional investments as well as real estate in order to maximize our returns.

Your retirement plan is a long-term investment, and over the long-term, real estate investments normally provide excellent returns. The bargain basement prices we are experiencing today can turn into a significant profit over 5 to 10 years for the savvy investor. As a CPA, I can show how this can be accomplished, including the tax-free manner in which it can be achieved. A real estate IRA offers the potential for exceptional returns, diversification to your plan, and a relatively low-risk over the long-term.

A self-directed or real estate IRA allows you to invest in various real estate holdings including, but not limited to:

- Single-family homes
- Multi-unit homes
- Apartment buildings
- Condominiums
- Commercial property
- Improved or unimproved land

That certainly provides a lot of potential in the real estate market, especially considering the bargain-basement prices that are available.

UNPRECEDENTED REAL ESTATE OPPORTUNITIES

Some would say that buying foreclosed homes and undervalued properties is capitalizing on the misfortune of others. We disagree. Sure, the present opportunities allow for a much more lucrative return over the long-term which is why we invest in them. However, many economists point out that if we are ever to truly reverse the country's economic turmoil, then we must clear the excess of unsold homes nationwide. Homes falling into disrepair across our country are not going to help pull us out of the economic problems we are facing. Producing wealth from these properties will, and that's what we do. It gives us the opportunity to revitalize neighbourhoods and at the same time...we take pride in that.

As a nation, we've been able to use a self-directed or real estate IRA to purchase investment property since 1974. A large segment of the population is unaware that this type of investment is available although that is rapidly changing. As I mentioned earlier, most financial advisors are keeping this investment option under wraps to protect their revenue streams from traditional investments – even when those investments are taking the beating they are now.

Many new retirees are becoming aware of the benefits of a self-directed IRA, and 75% of them are rolling their 401k into one to capitalize on the diversification it provides. This is good news for new retirees as they can now search the investment marketplace based on the value it offers. If it's a strategy that current retirees are taking advantage of, imagine the wealth a real-estate IRA can provide over 30, 40, or 50 years. All with tax-free benefits.

A real estate or self-directed IRA offers you:

- A solid, diversified retirement plan to weather fluctuating returns in the investment marketplace.
- A long-term investment strategy that has traditionally delivered high returns.
- The opportunity to increase your investment income by purchasing significantly undervalued real estate.
- Tax-deferred rental income.
- The ability to reinvest the tax-free income into more real estate opportunities or other traditional investments.
- The ability to protect the proceeds from capital gains tax when selling an income property.

HOW THE INVESTMENT PROGRAM WORKS

Lisa and I have spent several years streamlining our real estate investment program. Our goal has always been to produce exceptional results for all participants involved in the transaction. The result is a program that offers you solid returns, low-risk, and the opportunity to grow your retirement nest egg as a real estate investor. We generally:

- Work with private investors such as yourself.
- Produce returns that are double or triple bank CD rates.
- Buy undervalued properties, renovate them if necessary, rent them out, and hold on to them as an appreciable asset until its time to sell.
- Help you navigate the complexities of the Internal Revenue Code to ensure you are aware of the IRS compliance issues involved.

Our program uses private investors to buy undervalued properties. Why private investors? We require the flexibility to move swiftly when we spot a profitable property. By the time it takes us to go through the approval process of a bank or mortgage lender, the property can be snapped up by another investor. Besides, lenders took a bath on home mortgages and are reluctant to provide funds without performing an in-depth due diligence. We don't have that kind of time.

We also cut out the middlemen in these transactions and avoid or reduce real estate commissions, mortgage broker fees, loan broker fees, and property management charges. These cost savings are better served in your account, don't you agree?

When we are scrutinizing a potential real estate transaction, we look at producing a minimum of $20,000 profit. If we cannot realize that amount then we pass on the opportunity. Our private lenders currently earn 2 to 3 times bank rates, usually 7% to 9% on our real estate-secured notes. Monthly payments of principal and interest are offered or you can choose to receive just the interest and keep the principal working for you.

You won't find any hidden fees or commissions; we lay out our real estate investment opportunity for your scrutiny. Our policy is to only borrow up to 65% of the value of the property from private lenders to provide an equity cushion that helps secure your investment. Our private lenders are secured with a first mortgage on the property. Title insurance is provided in addition to being named on the Hazard insurance policy for additional peace of mind. To add icing on the cake, these private mortgages are fully transferable and can be passed down to your heirs.

YOU MAY NOT SEE ANOTHER OPPORTUNITY LIKE THIS IN YOUR LIFETIME

The winds of change are shifting and the economy is taking tentative steps towards recovery. As the economy improves, house prices will begin to rise again. This is great news for us as our current holdings will provide higher returns. But the longer you wait to take advantage of these truly exceptional real estate deals, the less profit you'll be able to realize. The longer you wait the less chance you'll have to build a significant retirement fund that will take care of you during your senior years.

Lisa and I would love for you to become a part of our team. We don't want you to be one of the retirement statistics we mentioned above. The real estate investment opportunities that we are experiencing today may never be seen again. Contact us today to learn how you can experience significant returns as a private investor in our real estate program.

ABOUT RICK

Rick and Lisa Donner's story starts out pretty normal. Rick is originally from western Pennsylvania, and Lisa is from Miami. Rick is a CPA in Fort Myers, FL with a practice that has a concentration in real estate investing. Lisa has been an entrepreneur and has owned and managed several businesses. She began a women's real estate investing group in April 2007 which has an average attendance of 50.

Rick and Lisa have successfully bought and sold numerous properties over the last several years helping both those who need to sell and those who want to buy. They currently focus on quick turning single family houses and holding multi-family and commercial properties. As Real Estate Coaches and Mentors, Rick and Lisa teach their students how to become successful real estate investors using various techniques and strategies based on current market conditions. In other words, what's working now and how you can apply it to make money. The Donners are also Mentors for Ron LeGrand's Millionaire Mentorship Program, having students both throughout the U.S. and internationally. As believers in multiple streams of income, they have several successful businesses in addition to their Real Estate Investing and CPA businesses.

To learn more about The Donners, and how you can make Gobs of Money Now using Real Estate IRA's, get your FREE Report when you visit their websites at www.CPANationalFunding.com and at: www.DonnerCPA.com or call 1-239-590-9144.

CHAPTER 17

THE 11 CRUCIAL STEPS THEY WON'T TELL YOU ON TV THAT YOU *REALLY* NEED ... TO GET STARTED IN REAL ESTATE

by Ricky Strain

Want to get started in Real Estate investing? If you are watching the TV or listening to the radio, of course you do. You will be rich in no time with little to no effort according to the infomercials and radio ads. Just go to the FREE seminar next Saturday and you will be ready to go. However, it's not quite that easy and it costs a lot more than that. It is a great time to get into the real estate market, but, where do you start and how do you go about it?

Let me give you some things to think about and then I will give you an outline that will be meaningful and useful to getting you started in the right direction.

The first thing you need to answer for yourself is WHY you want to get into real estate investing. The "why" is first and foremost. If the why isn't big enough and compelling enough, you will bail when things get tough, and they will. You need a very clear understanding of why you want to do this.

How committed are you to making this work? Are you willing to turn the TV off, give up the mall, fishing, golf, etc.? Real Estate is not a pastime or part time job if you want to be successful. You are not going to get rich quick, period. I don't care what all of the guru's tell you. It is going to take money and it is going to take time.

Do you have the money to get the necessary training to get a good start in whatever area of real estate you would like to concentrate on. If you don't pay for the training up front, you will pay for it later as you make mistakes that can cost you hundreds if not thousands of dollars. You can go to all of the free seminars you want, but I guarantee you will not walk away with the knowledge to do the business.

How do you pick someone to work with whom you can trust to teach you what you need to know without paying 'an arm and a leg'? There are 100's of people out there that are telling you they have the way to the real estate 'pot of gold.' It is like traveling to a foreign country that you have never seen and they speak a language you have never heard. It is a lost and helpless feeling.

Do you have steady income now that can sustain you while you are working your way into the real estate arena? If you do that's great. This will minimize the pressure on you as you get the real estate business up and running. The last thing you want to do is to give that up before you have money coming in Real Estate. More businesses fail in the first 12 months because of a lack of capital than for any other single reason. In a new startup business, cash flow is everything.

I am not trying to paint an ugly picture, be a devil's advocate, or a 'dream stealer.' I want you to go in with your eyes open. Real Estate is a great business to be in. It has, in fact, made many people wealthy over time. I can't imagine not being in the market. It is exciting, rewarding and a lot of fun. You can help a lot of people when you buy and sell in many ways. You can provide owner financing to those who can't get a loan because of bad credit. You can help people who are headed to foreclosure by purchasing their house before they lose it. You can help banks move the properties that they have foreclosed on and want 'off' their books. It is all about providing solutions for property owners both in residential and commercial real estate.

Here are the steps I recommend you follow:-

1. Write down why you want to get into real estate and how long you are going to stay with it before 'throwing in the towel.' Are you looking for supplemental income, monthly cash flow or ultimately a full time job. I strongly suggest that if your time line is less than 12 months, you should consider something else.

2. How many dollars are you willing to set aside for the business in year 1 and be specific on where those dollars will go;
   a. Training
   b. Marketing
   c. Travel
   d. Investing

3. Decide if you want to focus on commercial or residential. Most people new to real estate feel more comfortable with residential because there are fewer zeros in the deals. For example, you might pick up a house for $10,000 but a nice commercial property could be $500,000 or more. The actual cost to get into the two deals might be the same, but the numbers scare people away from the commercial deal. This is also why there is less competition for commercial deals. One advantage of investing in residential is that there are some laws affording you some protection from unscrupulous parties. In Commercial Real Estate you are on your own.

4. Join your local Real Estate Investment Group (REIA). This will be a good group to network with, and possibly even partner with. They also have guest speakers that will provide you with some of your basic training.

5. Find a good real estate attorney who focuses 100% on real estate. Your local REIA, local investors, and Title companies will know who the good attorneys are. Make sure your attorney reviews every real estate document you use. He will keep you out of trouble from a legal standpoint.

6. Find a real estate guru who you like and feel you can trust to follow. This is the most important and the most difficult

step. If you know someone who is successful in real estate, find out who they use for their training. Take your time and be thorough here. You are looking for the top 10% here. Too many of the professed gurus are teachers who have not done deals, so they are giving you what they think works. Don't work with anyone who isn't doing deals right now.

7. Start your training. The most important areas are:-
    a. Take a basic course in the area you want to start. Keep in mind there are areas that return cash very quickly and other areas that are longer term.
       i. If you need cash right away, I suggest taking a course on wholesaling ("Flipping"). You will get junk houses under contract and then sell them to other investors who like to rehab them. You should only need a few dollars to complete one of these transactions.
       ii. If you have money to invest you have several more options. You can go to auctions such as REDC, you can buy bank owned (REO) properties with good discounts from Realtors or directly from the banks, you can buy at foreclosure auctions, and you can work on short sales just to name a few. These options are all cash strategies.
    b. Get very good at whatever area you choose. Jumping around is a formula for failure early on. Find your niche and get very good at it before you add another strategy.
8. Get your marketing cranked up. You've got to have prospects. You should learn the specific marketing strategies for the niche you have chosen. Make sure the training you choose includes marketing.
9. You need to form an LLC, Limited Liability Company. You need to do this because you never want to take ownership in your own name, never. Your real estate attorney should be able to help you with this. It will cost about $200-$300 dollars. You can go on line and do it yourself if you like and save a little.
10. MAKE OFFERS! You have got to make offers. This is where you have to overcome your fears and take action. I have found that this is where most "newbie's" fail because they cannot

pull the trigger. You cannot buy if you don't try. A mentor can be a big help here but they cost. Most mentoring programs start around $10,000. This is a decision you have to make. If you lack the confidence to do it on your own, a mentor could be the thing that makes the difference.

11. Always follow up. Follow up separates the winners and losers. Running your marketing campaign to get the phone to ring and not returning the calls doesn't get deals done. You would be surprised at how many 'wannabe' investors will not return the calls. You will also find that situations change. What was not a deal today, could very well be a 'killer' deal tomorrow. This is especially true with distressed properties. The closer it gets to some financial deadline, the more negotiable the parties become. Examples of financial deadlines are pending bankruptcy, foreclosure auction, and a balloon payment coming due, to name a few.

The real estate business is about knowledge, contacts and perseverance. One good deal in real estate can bring in more money than a lot of people can make at a normal 9-5 job in a year. This is the allure. Just realize that one good deal doesn't happen by accident or luck. It does happen by following the outline I have given you along with a lot of hard work. You will find out that the harder you work at this, the luckier you get!

A couple of other areas I would like to mention but not go into detail at this time are asset protection and qualified retirement accounts such as Roth IRA's, 401 K's, and HSA's. It is important to protect, preserve, and maximize your real estate profits as they begin to come in. You can actually purchase real estate inside of certain retirement accounts, thereby deferring taxes or in some cases completely eliminating them. Equity Trust is one company that understands and specializes in these types of retirement accounts. You can find them at: www.TrustETC.com. There are many, many asset protection lawyers out there. Please do not ignore these areas if you want to keep most of what you earn in this business.

I personally focus on distressed properties, both commercial and residential. I have been very successful doing this but realize I have spent a lot of money and time with many gurus to get where I am today. I have had several mentors to keep me on track and keep me motivated. I participate in real estate Mastermind Groups where we share ideas and successes. I am a graduated Master of Real Estate with one of the top Gurus in the country. I spend $50k to $100k per year for training, every year. The market changes, the laws change, and even the techniques can change. You have to keep your education current. I could not have progressed this far this fast without the unselfish help of many other real estate investors and gurus.

I am very active in distressed commercial real estate and have done many multimillion dollar deals for myself and others. I have a formal program where I help others participate in commercial deals regardless of their experience level. I teach them how to find the deals and then I get the deals done for them. This includes negotiating the deal, funding the deal and cashing out the deal. My partners are never out of pocket and never at risk. I take all of the risk and fund all of the deal. I don't think you will find many people in this business that will do the same. If you are looking for a short cut in commercial and have limited knowledge and resources I can help. You can join my team at: www. RSPropertyScoutsUSA.com. I focus on deals in the $500K to $5M range. I have a similar program for distressed residential properties. If you would like to find out more about that program you can email me at: RStrain@RSInvestmentConcepts.com.

You should get your training in and learn as much as you can, regardless of how you proceed in the real estate arena. You can never have too much knowledge and that is the one thing that no one can take from you. Invest in yourself, find someone you trust and let them help you stay motivated and accountable.

Become a part of a Mastermind Group when you can afford to. Being a part of a Mastermind Group allows you to hang with highly motivated winners. There is nothing like being in a room with winners. You won't find 'dream stealers' inside this group. I sometimes have openings in my groups, so you can contact me if you would be interested in joining my TEAM.

ABOUT RICKY

Ricky A Strain began his career in manufacturing with a Bachelor of Science in Mechanical Engineering from Rose-Hulman Institute of Technology and a Professional Engineering License from the State of Indiana. He spent 25 years building, starting up and operating manufacturing plants throughout the US and Mexico. This included land acquisition, plant and equipment design and construction, and the hiring and training of personnel.

In the 80's he bought and sold single family residential properties as a Realtor and as an investor.

Ricky relocated with his family to Gainesville, Florida from Mexico in 2001, where he resides now.

Ricky was Director of Operations for a large home builder in the State of Florida 2005-2006 in a turnaround situation. He restructured, hired and trained a new group of people to accomplish the needed changes. There were significant improvements in quality and cost.

In 2008 he decided to start up RS Investment Concepts to capitalize on the opportunities that were emerging in real estate and to help others do the same. He and his team are actively pursuing the acquisition of distressed properties. This includes short sales, foreclosures, Bank owned properties, non-performing bank assets, and commercial properties.

He has been trained extensively in real estate wholesaling, retailing, rehabbing, finance, marketing, commercial, bulk REO's, probate, property management, asset protection, tax liens and deeds.

Ricky is a Master and a Master Mind with Ron LeGrand and also follows other marketing and real estate gurus such as Robert Kiyosaki, Bill Walsh, George Miller, David Lindahl, Wayne Gray, Cameron Dunlap, Bill Duquette, Alan Cowgill, Sal Buscemi, Bill Glazer, Dan Kennedy, Duncan Weirman, Bonnie Laslo, and Bryan Ellis.

Investor support groups are being established in 2010 to help other investors succeed. Ricky is helping with marketing, deal analysis, funding and acquisition. He is also a member of the North Florida Real Estate Investors Association and the Hobby Millionaires.

Ricky is the Chief Operating Officer for Pinnacle Commercial Group, LLC., a company that specializes in the acquisition of and the "Adding of Value" to Distressed and Defaulted "Recession Resistant" Commercial assets throughout the United States.

CHAPTER 18
CATCHING THE GIANT WAVE!

by Tom Burtness

"It's not possible! It can't be done!" The distant roar muffled the complaints of Buzzy Kerbox and Darrick Doerner.

"Yes, it can," insisted Laird Hamilton. "Just because we haven't surfed it before doesn't mean it can't be done!"

The film documentary *Riding Giants* follows the journey of Doerner, Hamilton, and Kerbox overcoming both external obstacles and inner fears on their way to becoming masters of the giant wave. Just as their breakthrough to success required a team, so we can experience the same leaps forward when we draw on a qualified real-estate mentor.

The three bronzed, athletic, 'twenty-something' surfers squinted through their binoculars at the mountainous waves that hammered the North Shore of Hawaii's third reef. Doerner, Hamilton, and Kerbox were addicted to the adrenaline rush of big-wave surfing. But these waves were different. They brought fear and awe. These were not the routine twenty- to thirty-foot breakers that big-wave surfers around the world routinely tested their mettle against. No, these were eighty-foot monsters of unimaginable power that for decades surfers could see, but not touch; feel, but not ride. No one had ever conquered waves this size. Doerner, Hamilton, and Kerbox had watched a few risk-takers try and had seen some die in the attempt.

Could this be the impenetrable barrier, the limit to human possibility? Conventional wisdom, experience, and history said so. But these three men saw the awesome possibility. They believed that someone would master these invincible behemoths. And they wanted to be the ones that were remembered for achieving the ultimate victory.

THE WOULD-BE MASTERS

In my thirty-five years as an engineer, contractor and real estate entrepreneur, I have known dozens of people who have peered into the real-estate world and wanted to be a part of it. They saw the possibilities. They believed it could be done. They saw others accomplishing great things and wanted to be a part of it. But they also saw others try and fail in the attempt. They were in awe of the potential rewards, but the tales of people crashing and drowning in the real-estate industry kept them paralyzed in fear 'on the shore.'

Perhaps you've dreamed of being a part of the real-estate world, financially successful beyond anything that you have previously achieved. What barriers keep you from diving into the water? What fears keep you on the shore? What conventional wisdom has beached you? How could you become one of the people who achieve the thrill of victory? How can you find a way to break through your limitations to fulfill your dreams?

THE BREAKTHROUGH

Doerner, Hamilton, and Kerbox were confident they could surf the eighty-foot waves. That wasn't the problem. The limitations to their success revolved around one problem: getting started. They could not paddle themselves fast enough to catch those waves. They knew that as the size of the wave increases, so does its speed. They simply did not have the physical strength to get moving fast enough in the right place to catch the giant waves. And if they failed to catch one, the next wave would pound them with deadly force.

One December day in 1992, these three entrepreneurial adventurers, bored with the thirty-footers that were challenging the rest of the mop-head crowd at Sunset Beach, began pulling each other around on their surfboards behind a Jet Ski. Like kids with a new toy, they experimented with as many ways as they could find to jump and play with the waves. In the midst of a particularly awesome wake jump, an unexpected thought struck Laird. "I'm going fast, really fast. Probably fast enough to catch one of the giants."

Within hours they had hatched a plot to give their newfound revelation a try on the unridden realm of the Peahi break on Maui's North Shore. By dusk the following day, Doerner, Hamilton, and Kerbox had invented the whole new sport of Tow-In Surfing. They could tow each other fast enough behind the Jet Ski to get to the exact right spot at the perfect speed to catch the monster waves. They had conquered the giants! Suddenly, the limitation that had prevented their success was destroyed; the barrier was gone and success was theirs.

What made the difference? The key element was the person on the Jet Ski. That person could do for them what they could not do for themselves. He could tow them to the right spot at the right time and the right speed so they could conquer the giant wave without being crushed. In so doing, they would experience a thrill that other people only dreamt about.

In real estate, your "person on the Jet Ski" is your mentor.

BOTH TEACHING AND TRAINING ARE NEEDED

We need to understand the difference between teaching and training. These days, infomercials and many other sources offer teaching to get you into the real-estate business. Some is good, and some is not so good.

The first step is sorting through the available options so that you are hearing only good teaching. There are a lot of talking heads who don't know how to practice what they're preaching. You need to learn from someone who is doing the stuff and producing results. For several years now, I have been learning from Ron Legrand. I consider his teaching excellent because it works. My bank account proves it!

However, simply hearing awesome real-estate teaching does not make you money. Correct action does. True learning happens when I get to the place where I can do what it is that I've been taught. Training is the process of turning correct ideas into correct action. So, we need both teaching and training.

Mentors assist us in this process. My mentor is the person who takes good teaching and helps me turn it into training in several specific ways. First, he or she helps me make the paradigm shifts that I need in order to have correct ideas and thoughts. Second, my mentor helps me know what to do, what not to do, and in what order; and holds me accountable to do it. Third, my mentor helps me break through the barriers in my mind and emotions that keep me from success. Correct ideas, correct actions, and correct attitudes.

Remember, my mentor is not there to do it for me, to make me do something, or to make decisions for me. My mentor is there to help me with the thoughts that I need to have and decisions that I need to make, in order to take correct action. I am responsible for my own decisions, but my mentor has the experience to guide me as I make them.

CORRECT IDEAS - WE NEED PARADIGM SHIFTS

One of the most challenging parts of being a mentor is understanding and assisting my students with the paradigm shifts that they need in order to think the right thoughts. People will take action according to what they really believe – their paradigms – regardless of what they've been taught. Our mentor's job is to watch what we do, determine what our real paradigms are, and help us to adjust them. Allow me to give you some examples of paradigms that must be shifted in order for a real-estate investor to be successful.

False Paradigm Number 1: The Traditional Retail System Paradigm

Many people are familiar with the traditional retail real-estate system where a seller goes to a real-estate agent and lists their property on the MLS. A network of agents and brokers then attract buyers and negotiate offers. The agents negotiate between the seller and buyer to complete a sale using MLS forms and procedures after which the seller pays a commission that is divided between the seller's agent and the buyer's agent. This system is effective for retail real estate, but it also creates several distinct paradigms that are false for investors. For example:

1. The only way to buy or sell a house is through the traditional retail system.
2. The only "fair" amount of money to be made from a real-estate transaction is a 6 percent commission.
3. The only forms that can be used in a transaction are

MLS forms.

4. All forms that are used by MLS must be used or the transaction is not legal.
5. Licensed real-estate agents must be involved in all real-estate transactions.
6. All real estate transactions take several months to accomplish.
7. Buyers can't talk directly to sellers, only through real estate agents.

False Paradigm Number 2: Commission Instead of Profit

The big money in real estate is made from the difference in price between the amount that a property is bought for and what it sells for. This is called profit. The traditional retail system would lead you to believe that 6 percent is the highest fair amount to make on a real-estate transaction. However, in a free-market economy, the value of any good or service is the price that a willing buyer agrees to pay a willing seller. If a real-estate investor is able to buy a property from a willing seller for $20,000, and then the investor is able to sell that property to a different willing buyer for $30,000, the difference is a profit of $10,000. This is a totally ethical, legitimate, legal, and appropriate transaction, and it's far more profitable than the $1,200 - $1,800 that a 6 percent commission represents.

False Paradigm Number 3: It Takes Money to Make Money

"It takes money to make money." How many times have you heard that supposedly sage piece of wisdom? This age-old lie has 'beached' many would-be real estate entrepreneurs! If you believe it, you'll act on it. And you'll never see any of the many possibilities that exist for buying real estate without using any of your own money.

False Paradigm Number 4: No One Will Sell You Their House for Less Than Retail Price

It is virtually impossible for those steeped in the traditional real-estate paradigm to comprehend the myriad of reasons why someone would sell their house for far below appraised value, but that doesn't make those reasons any less valid. Perhaps a house needs significant renovations and the owner has no money to pay for those upgrades. Perhaps the owner lost his or her job and can no longer make mortgage payments, or perhaps he or she received a job promotion or relocation and has to move suddenly. Perhaps a parent who recently passed away owned the house and the new owners live in a distant state. Whatever the particular circumstances are, there are many people who will happily sell their house for less than retail price.

False Paradigm Number 5: The Only Houses You Can Buy Are Listed in MLS

Over the past three years, approximately 90 percent of the houses that my investment company has purchased were not listed on the MLS. As a matter of fact, in a majority of the cases, the owner was not even trying to sell the house before we contacted them!

As you can see from these examples, there are numerous false paradigms that may keep us from being successful real estate investors. This is where having a qualified mentor will keep us on track. They will hear what we say, watch what we do, and then give us feedback that allows us to correct our false ideas. Without this help, we can easily drown in the 'waves of ignorance.'

CORRECT ACTION - WHAT TO DO

In the many real-estate workshops, short courses and seminars I've attended, I have been exposed to a myriad of facts, techniques, and secrets. I usually go home from these educational experiences with my head spinning! Out of all the wonderful techniques I learned, where do I start? I need to know *what to do* and *what not to waste my valuable time on*. I also need to know in what order to apply the techniques. I need help to sort through the innumerable details to know which particular ones are necessary for me to succeed.

This is where my mentor comes in. Remember, my mentor's role is to help put me at the right location on the wave, at the right speed, at the right time. My mentor will help me know which techniques I need to implement first, and which need to wait for a future time.

CORRECT ATTITUDE - OVERCOMING EMOTIONAL AND MENTAL BARRIERS

No one will become a successful real-estate investor without learning to deal with the disbelievers, naysayers, and 'dream-stealers.' Uninformed people are everywhere, and they think they know what they're talking about. They say things like:

"It can't be done."
"You can't buy a house with no money."
"You can only borrow money from a bank."
"No one will sell you their house for less than it would appraise for."
"You can't do that without a real-estate license."

These kinds of thoughts can keep you ignorant, unhappy, and poor! Your mentor will help you recognize that your opportunity for success in real estate is available because other people don't know how to do what we know how to do.

Unfortunately, most real estate agents don't even understand the world of real-estate investment. In their ignorance and insecurity, they may attempt to intimidate us into thinking that what we are doing is inappropriate, immoral, or perhaps even illegal. Nothing could be further from the truth! We are simply buying and selling property at prices offered to us by the free market, and in the process we help some 'hurting' people out of whatever crisis they are in.

We must also break through mental and emotional barriers in order to be successful. Some of these barriers are a result of what we were taught as we were growing up… some are because the established system wants to keep us out… some are just from a lack of experience. All of these barriers must be conquered. Your mentor will help you to see in yourself what you cannot see, and help you overcome your limitations.

SURF'S UP!

We all know that today's high unemployment rate combined with the mortgage crisis is causing an immense wave of foreclosures from 'upside-down' properties. Current values are low. Supply is at an all time high. We feel empathy toward those who are caught in difficult personal circumstances, but as entrepreneurs, we recognize that this is the greatest real-estate opportunity in a generation!

By universal acclaim, Laird Hamilton is the greatest big-wave surfer in history. "The reason I'm able to ride the waves the way I do," Laird said, "is that I have partners like Dave and Darrick. I'm only arriving at this level because I'm being driven by these guys … Team is the key to success."

The surf is up! Do you see it? Do you dream of it? Do you want it? This is the moment to experience the thrill of success for those who are properly trained, and who have a skilled mentor to team up with them to help catch their giant wave! If you truly want to be a "New Master of Real Estate," find yourself a qualified mentor to tow you into the action. If you do, you'll experience the thrill of a lifetime!

References
Riding Giants. Directed by Stacy Peralta. Performed by Laird Hamilton, Greg Holl and Jeff Clark. 2004.

ABOUT TOM

Tom Burtness has been an adventurer his entire life, relentlessly pursuing the optimum approach to conquering the challenging waves in his own life, family, and career. He is an entrepreneur to the core. Tom has founded over twenty successful businesses and organizations in the past thirty-five years in a wide diversity of fields - ranging from consulting engineering, construction, and real estate businesses, to a theatre production company and a church.

Tom is passionate about helping people find and realize the vision for their lives, families and businesses. Dubbed a "mentor of mentors," Tom served as director for North and Central America for a distance-learning institute that provides masters-level business leadership training. In this role, Tom oversaw an international network of over two hundred mentors, and taught seminars, short courses and in-service training events in Canada, Costa Rica, Guatemala, and throughout the Unites States.

His teaching and writing style blends both the "why" and the "how-to." Tom possesses a rare ability to see both the philosophy behind a principle and the way to live it out; it has been said of Tom that he is a "bridge between the theoretical and the practical." Tom finds it curiously ironic that his engineering specialization of illumination design parallels his passion to assist his students in achieving practical "illumination" to excel in their fields of endeavor.

Tom and his wife of more than thirty-five years, Emily, carry their passion for mentoring into their family life as well. They home educated their four children from grade school through graduation from high school. The three older children have all graduated from college with honors. Erick is a CFA, Kristiana is an editor and screenwriter, Michelle assists in their real-estate business, and Hannah is studying graphic design at the University of Illinois.

Tom extends his love for taking calculated risks into his leisure activities as well. He has enjoyed many years of the excitement involved in off-road motorcycling, scuba diving, downhill skiing, rock climbing and rappelling, and being a private pilot. Tom is a long distance runner and completed three half-marathon events last year. His personal motto is "Never stop adventuring!"

Tom currently co-owns and runs four businesses, including a real estate investment business with his son-in-law, Zach Morrison; a real estate investment capital funding business; an investment advisor firm; and a green energy residential improvements business. Tom can be reached at: tom@illinihomebuyers.com. He and Emily reside near Champaign-Urbana, Illinois and are avid fans of the University of Illinois. Go Illini!

CHAPTER 19
SEEING THE FORTUNE
THROUGH THE WEEDS!

by Troy Singer

O h, this is going to be exciting! I have one Chapter and about 2,500 words to introduce you to a concept, which, if fully embraced, could net you an extra $100,000 in the next 12 months. Let me also mention you can do this in your spare time, 'under the radar', while paying attention to the 'hidden gems' you've been driving by every day, until now. And the best part about this, you can truly do this using much more of your mind and sweat equity while leaving your money in your back pocket. Does this sound too good to be true? I admit it does. But it doesn't make the concept invalid or an idea you shouldn't get hyped about. What is it do you ask?... Its *Vacant Houses*!

Let me say from the very beginning that this will not be a PhD dissertation. I don't have the word space or the "Professor Status" to give to you all the finite details of this investment strategy. I suggest you look to the guru in the business if you connect with the idea I'm about to share. Ever since I was personally introduced to this idea early in my investment pursuits by my teachers, Ron LeGrand and Cameron Dunlap, I knew this would be a big part of my business. It's the favorite part of my business, and in my opinion, one of the least difficult ways to get into the Real Estate investment game.

The best part about learning to invest in *Vacant Houses* is that you can implement repeatable processes that would make netting $10,000 a month very achievable - while getting in and out of these houses quickly and without leaving your name on a trail of houses all over your city. The basics are simple and I'll touch on them quickly. I'll discuss identifying properties and prospects, locating and contacting owners, structuring and presenting the deal, acquiring and selling properties to get paid! Again, this will be the 'Cliff Notes' version, with hopes you'll run out and get the novel. Sooooooo ...if you are intrigued to learn more, let's begin.

INDENTIFYING PROSPECTS

The beauty of working with *Vacant Houses* is that every neighborhood has them. For this chapter I'll define *Vacant Houses* as homes that are not currently lived in and are not listed with a realtor or currently for sale. Of course lower to middle income communities have more of these vacant houses than 'high end' neighborhoods. Some vacant houses are very apparent they're vacant and ignored while others aren't as easily identified as vacant. From people having to move suddenly because of unforeseen circumstances to landlords who are torn between wanting to continue to be a landlord, vacant houses are all around you, and I challenge you to search them out as opportunities.

I have three main ways that I identify vacant houses. By driving neighborhoods myself, sending out others to drive neighborhoods, and by following up on returned mail from mailings I send out in other aspects of my Real Estate investing. The first two are very similar to one another, with the only difference of who does the house hunting. I'll briefly explain the third however that probably relates more to other strategies discussed in this book.

Let's talk about driving neighborhoods; I love it, setting aside 3 to 4 hours on a weekend with my favorite XM radio presets on deck and a city map to follow. I then turn up the music and start hunting for properties. I choose neighborhoods that have entry level first time buyer type homes with decent to good school systems. This would be the basic 3 bedroom, 1 to 2 bath homes that are affordable and desirable to the average small families. Its imperative you don't choose to start with 'high end' neighborhoods. You'll find more vacant houses in neighborhoods affordable to the average first time homebuyer.

Signals that a house is vacant vary from very mild and unnoticeable to overly blatant. You're looking for houses that look like they're being ignored. Overgrown bushes and grass, piled up newspapers, houses with no curtains and no furniture. Some houses will have stickers or sheets on their front doors stating they are vacant or winterized. The best time to go vacant house hunting is a day or two after it snows. Houses without shoveled, walked-through or driven-in driveways, or foot tracks to the front door could very well be vacant. You'll be surprised how intuitive you'll become at identifying vacant homes with some practice.

Once you identify a *vacant house*, it's time to take out a camera and take a few pictures to document the house. Take a picture of the front and back of the house as well as the backyard and the neighbor houses on either side especially if they are 'junky.' You also want to note the condition of the house and any obvious repairs that you can identify from the outside or by looking into the windows. [For noting the condition, please contact me at troy@swohiohomesolutions.com for an official inspection sheet to use.]

The second way to identify *vacant houses* is to send someone else out to do the house hunting. [In the business, they are also referred to as birddogs.] If driving around new neighborhoods isn't quite your cup of tea, then you can always hire someone to do so. You can pay someone $5 to $10 per *vacant house* found using the same criteria I've described earlier. Although I've found plenty of people in my in my friendship circle willing to do this, I've heard Craigslist is an excellent place to find birddogs. I also recommend making sure you pay them as an independent contractor and not an employee. Be very clear of the criteria each vacant house lead has to meet - in order to be paid on. This includes minimal information and pictures of the property. This information should be given to you within 48 hours of being obtained. Using birddogs is an excellent way of covering a larger area of your town in a shorter amount of time. Whether you drive neighborhoods yourself or use birddogs, identifying *vacant houses* is the easiest part of my system.

LOCATING AND CONTACTING OWNERS

Now that you have *vacant houses* as prospects to purchase, the next step is to locate and contact the property owners. Your first stop should be your county property search site. In Ohio, the property searches I use are at the county auditor's website. It will provide the name and mailing address of the owner of the house. Most of the houses will be listed as being owned by an individual owner, but a growing number will be listed as owned by either the government or a bank. For this article, I'll speak only to houses owned by individuals.

Once I have the owner's information, I then send a letter to them at the mailing address letting them know I'm interested in purchasing their vacant house. [Hint: Endorse the outside of the envelope with the term "Address Service Requested" in order to have the owners forwarded address sent back to you if they've moved, or have the *vacant house* as their mailing address.]

In addition to sending letters to the listed owner, at the same time I research the owner's telephone number. I use the phonebook, Internet search sites, neighbors or you can run a Skip Trace. The site that I use is: www.findtheseller.com which specializes in finding home owners for Real Estate investors. It's owned by Cameron Dunlap, who is one of my mentors. Yes, it's all in the family.

Please know that it typically takes a few letters and phone calls to get to a seller. Don't give up too soon. The payoff is in the persistence. Also, regarding bank and government owned properties; you can find direction regarding how to handle this at both www.ronlegrand.com and www.camerondirect.com.

CONSTRUCTING OFFERS TO YOUR SELLERS

After you identify and engage the owner, it's time to make an offer. When it comes to being successful in the *vacant house* business, there are two things you need to always keep in mind. Never pay more than "MAO" and "Buy low then sell low."

MAO stands for Maximum Allowable Offer. To determine MAO, you need to verify what the After Repair Market Value is [ARV]. And to get to the true ARV you'll need to get some good comparables to houses that have recently sold near the vacant house you are interested in. Once you have your ARV determined now you can calculate MAO. (ARV - 35%) - Needed Repairs = MAO. For example, if your ARV is $100,000 and your needed repairs totals $15,000, your MAO is $50,000. Again, you should pay no more than $50,000 for this house. Observing the MAO rule should not only go a long way to making sure you don't lose money on your investments, but also gives you plenty of room to create win-win situations with your buyers.

Depending on how much the current owner owes for the house will determine the type of offer you construct and present to them. If the current owner owns the house 'Free and Clear', then you can work with them directly offering them cash or creating an *owner financed* agreement with them. If they have an existing mortgage balance then you can offer to take over their mortgage "Subject To." [I'm thinking one of my friends will go into more detail about "Subject To" in another chapter.] And if the current owner is behind on their mortgage payments, then we can negotiate with their bank for a short sale.

The only constant is that we do our best to work directly with the current owner with no Real Estate Agents or Banks involved. This is where the term "Creative Real Estate" becomes real. Creating win-win situations outside of the norm is fun and rewarding for all.

SELLING THE PROPERTY AND GETTING PAID

If most of the rules were followed in constructing the offer to purchase the house, then realizing a profit will be easy once a viable exit strategy is executed. By following the rule of never paying more than MAO, you keep your exit strategies open. It allows you to have the repairs done, then sell the house to a owner-occupant buyer for a $20,000 to $30,000 profit on a home with a $100,000 ARV [Retailing] or what I currently do and recommend, selling to a local rehabber for $5,000 to $10,000 above MAO without dealing with the repairs [wholesaling]. That also enables the rehabber to earn a nice profit - which will keep him coming back for more deals in the future. This is where the "Buy low then sell low" philosophy comes in. Let's look at these two business strategies in a little more detail.

Retailing is the typical way that most people think of when they consider Real Estate investing or "flipping" houses. Buying, fixing-up and renting or selling to an owner-occupant. This can be a lucrative business for smart and experienced investors earning a net profit of at least

$20,000. For 'higher end' houses or houses in major cities, I've heard of six figure profits gained in deals and I say good for them! These profits are well deserved since there is a lot of work and risk that goes into a major rehab project for profit. Not to mention it's very easy to have 6 months to a year's worth of work in a property when considering fix up and possible time on market. Although this isn't my current preferred investment strategy, I do see the lure of the big paycheck. I will some-day take on a retailing project, but for now I prefer wholesaling.

Wholesaling is where you buy and sell, but with no 'fix ups' and very little time spent in the property. You use your *vacant house* hunting and negotiation skills to buy these houses at 65% of the After Repaired Value [ARV] or less, then sell the house for at least 70% of the ARV minus repairs. This ensures us a spread of at least 5% - which is a great profit for the wholesale business. Your target buyers are usually going to be rehabbers who are in the business of fixing up houses and selling them retail. They are always looking for bargains and I'm proposing that you systemize being able to provide a constant source of true bar-gains to them while making a small profit on each one. We're keeping the long term goal in mind by buying low and selling low. We're leav-ing plenty of profit on the table for our rehabber customers who hope-fully will become repeat customers and promote our bargain houses to others. These houses should be first-time homebuyer houses. The price range of this type of house varies from area to area but in my market of Dayton, Cincinnati and Columbus Ohio, I look for houses with an ARV between $80k and $140K for wholesale deals. Staying in the first-time home buyer range keeps both our customer [rehabber] and their cus-tomer [owner occupant] at its widest and the most affordable. Between the constant incentives available for first time homebuyers and constant dream in our great country to own your own home, there will always be a market for entry level homes that we can serve and benefit from.

CLOSING

There you go, if you weren't familiar with the *Vacant House* opportu-nities in your neighborhood or town, now you have no excuse. If any of this chapter made sense to you then I suggest you take action. My job was to introduce you to the concept that I love and find personally rewarding. Please know I am by no means the one you should count on for the 'nuts and bolts' of the strategies. For that I send you to my mentors Ron LeGrand: www.ronlegrand.com or Cameron Dunlap: www.camerondirect.com. Their knowledge is vast and their strategies are proven and worth the training expense. However you can always consider me a 'partner in crime' and a resource to discuss strategies and celebrate your wins. [www.troysinger.com]

Be well and to our success!

ABOUT TROY

Troy Singer is a native Ohioan who loves living in Dayton Ohio. His true passions are Real Estate investing, golf, traveling, running and exercising. Troy also enjoys serving on committees for the Dayton United Way and on the board of the Dayton Habitat for Humanity.

Troy was first introduced to Ron LeGrand and Real Estate investing in November 2007 in NYC. Since then, Troy has enthusiastically stayed within the wholesaling side of the business as a part-time investment and business venture.

In addition to Real Estate Investing, Troy is a trained sales professional with over 16 years experience in print and packaging sales. He currently works for the Hooven-Dayton Corp in a Relationship Manager role to the company's single largest customer. The Hooven-Dayton Corp is a label and flexible packaging printer in Dayton Ohio.

To contact Troy, visit: www.TroySinger.com or call him at (937) 694-4393

www.TroySinger.com

Free CD Order Form
of Ron LeGrand Interviews

As my way of saying thanks for buying this book I'd be pleased to send you any or all of the CD's below, each worth $19.95, a **total value of $79.80** for *only $12.95* S&H. But there's a catch. Not a big catch, just a small favor. All I ask is you tell your friends about my book and maybe a polite nudge to get them to buy.

Check all CD's you'd like to receive. The S&H is the same for one or all.

☐ **How You Can Be A Quick Turn Real Estate Millionaire Without Previous Experience**
This frank discussion with Mentor Magazine explores the lucrative world of quick turn real estate and where the really big money is made including behind the scenes secrets rarely disclosed elsewhere.

☐ **Everything You Ever Wanted To Know About Land Trusts**
This interview answers every question ever asked about how, why and when to use land trusts to buy real estate and discusses the risks you take if you don't.

☐ **How To Bomb Proof Your Assets**
This interview with a national attorney who specializes in asset protection, estate planning, tax reduction and entity structuring could save you a fortune and be the difference between keeping or losing a lifetime of wealth.

☐ **Where To Get The Money**
This interview explains where you can get all the money you'll need to buy and rehab properties regardless of your credit or financial condition. It contains the secrets banks don't want you to know and Ron explains how he got started with no money or credit and overcame bankruptcy to buy over 40 houses his first year.

Free CD Order Form
of Ron LeGrand Interviews

Please Print Clearly

Name: _____

Address: _____

City: _____ State: _____

Zip: _____

Phone: (____) _____Cell: (____) _____

Fax: (____) _____

Email: _____

Check Only One

Credit or Debit Card:

☐ Please charge credit card _____, exp. date _____

$12.95 for S&H.

ACH Payment or Bank Draft:

☐ Routing Number _____

Account Number _____

Authorized Signature _____

(Must have the information above. No P.O. Boxes please. S&H covers all CDs selected.)

1) *Order* online at **http://www.RonLeGrand.com/4FreeCDs**
2) *Fax* this completed order form to: **888-840-8385 or 904-262-1464** (24 hours/7 days a week)
3) *Mail* this completed order form with check to:
   Global Publishing, Inc. 9799 St. Augustine Road ,Jacksonville, FL 32257
4) *Call:* **1-888-843-8389** (M-F 9am ET-5pm ET)

Would you like to be a ☐ Full Time or ☐ Part Time investor?

What would you expect to make your first year?

_____

What would stop you?

_____

When would you like to start?

_____

How To Make An Absolute Fortune In A Slow Market Harvesting Foreclosure Gold

Did you know _we are in the middle of the biggest real estate gold rush in our lifetime_ and a lot of people are getting very rich, very fast by capitalizing on the foreclosure bonanza?

I'll give you my complete system on pre and post foreclosures in a manual with step-by-step instructions and 10 CDs of my 2 day seminar and a clear plan on what to do next, how to do it and how fast you can expect it to pay off.

Here are some of the things I covered in a simple, step-by-step format designed for beginners and pros alike in my two-day seminar.

- How to find killer deals not in the MLS and target only the best prospects.

- **How to prescreen in seconds any and all types of foreclosures whether they come with existing debt, one or two mortgages or if they are bank owned with no debt. This will allow you to get ten times more deals in a fraction of the time.**

- It's probably the biggest mistake most investors make...chasing dead ends.

- **How to raise the money to buy bank-owned houses one at a time or in big blocks, and how to invest capital you have to get 300% returns on cash, both inside and outside your IRA.**

- Short sales made simple, so you can instantly tell if it will be worth pursuing or not. This will save you months of wasted time pursuing short sales you should have known from day one were worthless.

- **What to offer on all-cash deals to absolutely guarantee you have a five-figure profit on quick flips you can do in a few days.**

- How to have an army of buyers waiting to take all the deeds off your hands you can find, and how you can set up a simple but automated system to flip junkers and never talk to your buyer.

- **How to get hundreds of thousands of dollars in free equity on houses before they go to the bank without risk to you.**

- How to buy your next residence with no down payment or credit, even if you've been through foreclosure yourself or are in bankruptcy. Your credit is irrelevant. No one will check it.

- **How to sell the houses quickly to create cash now, cash flow and big paydays months from now when you least expect them. You'll learn how to get free assets and turn them into cash. Try that in the stock market.**

There's never been a time like this, and there may never be again. **The rules are getting written daily, and the opportunities are so plentiful and vast,** it's no longer an issue of finding deals, it's more of a selection process of picking the ripest, low-hanging fruit. So fill out the form on the back of this page and get your **Fortunes In Foreclosures Home Study Course** shipped to your door now at our 80% discount as a new client.

Fortunes In Foreclosures Home Study Course
Order Form

Yes Ron! I'm ready to start on my path to my financial freedom with your **Fortunes In Foreclosures Home Study Course** *valued at $997.00 for only $197.00.* I understand it will be shipped immediately and it comes with a 60 day, unconditional money back guarantee if I'm not thrilled with it's content and the offer is good for 30 days.

Please Print Clearly

Name: _____

Address: _____

City: _____ State: _____ Zip: _____

Phone: (_____) _____ Cell: (_____) _____

Fax: _____ Email: _____

Florida Residents, sales tax will be added.

Check Only One

☐ <u>Credit or Debit Card:</u>

Please charge credit card _____, exp. date _____ $197 now.

OR

☐ <u>ACH Payment or Bank Draft:</u>

Check Number _____

Routing Number _____

Authorized Signature _____

(Must have the information above. No P.O. Boxes please.)

Order: online at **http://www.RonsForeclosureCourse.com**

Fax this completed order form to: **888-840-8385 or 904-262-1464** (24 hours/7 days a week)

Mail this completed order form with check to:

Global Publishing, Inc. 9799 St. Augustine Road Jacksonville, FL 32257